UNDERSTANDING THE UNITED METHODIST CHURCH

SECOND REVISED EDITION

by

Nolan B. Harmon

Nashville • ABINGDON PRESS • New York

UNDERSTANDING THE UNITED METHODIST CHURCH
SECOND REVISED EDITION

Library of Congress Cataloging in Publication Data

HARMON, NOLAN BAILEY, 1892-   Understanding the
    United Methodist Church.
    Published in 1955 and 1961 under title: Understanding
    the Methodist Church 1. United Methodist Church
    (United States)
    I. Title.
    BX8382.2.H35 1974   287'.6   73-20001
                ISBN 0-687-43005-4

MANUFACTURED BY THE PARTHENON PRESS AT
NASHVILLE, TENNESSEE, UNITED STATES OF AMERICA

*To every United Methodist who wants
to know more about his own church*

Foreword

To understand The United Methodist Church, one should know something about its:

HISTORY, and how it started
DOCTRINE, or what it believes
DISCIPLINE, or rules for conduct
ORGANIZATION, or how it works
WORSHIP and SACRAMENTS
ACTIVITIES and WORLD-WIDE PROGRAM
RELATION TO OTHER CHURCHES

In addition a United Methodist Christian will want to know how best one can fit into his church's life and in the hurried rush of present-day existence make time count more definitely for God and his Church. Written primarily for lay persons, this book will endeavor to explain United Methodism from the point of view of the local church.

A popular book of some years ago, *The Methodist Armor* by H. T. Hudson, suggested the general plan of this volume; and certain sentences and quotations from that book have been reproduced in these pages.

My interpretation of the Articles of Religion, the Confession of Faith, and the General Rules must stand on its own merit, though my treatment of these has been checked and approved by eminent authorities on United Methodist theology and life.

Understanding The United Methodist Church does not attempt to cover all important matters of life and law which are set forth in the *Book of Discipline* of The United Methodist Church. That book—the official book of doctrine, discipline, and law of the Church—should be in the homes of our people and may be referred to for many matters which necessarily could not be treated in this brief volume. Here the attempt has been made to interpret the *Discipline* in its most important provisions as well as to explain to present-day United Methodists many things which have to do with the practical working and high goal of their beloved Church.

Since the original publication of *Understanding the Methodist Church*, a notable organizational change has taken place with the creation of **The United Methodist Church.** This was the union of The Methodist and the Evangelical United Brethren Churches in 1968. To understand the United Methodist Church of today it is necessary to set forth something of the history and structure of both the Methodist and E.U.B. (as we commonly refer to it) connections and to indicate their mutual contributions to United Methodism. Happily these two church bodies, as we shall show, enjoyed a somewhat common origin, and since their union they are fulfilling as one communion the life and mission of a great Christian church. We trust that this book will be helpful both to those in the former Methodist Church and those in the former Evangelical and United Brethren Connections by giving them all a clearer understanding of their United Church. Bishop Hermann W. Kaebnick, of the former Evangelical United Brethren Church, is to be greatly thanked for carefully reading the entire manuscript of this book and for helping with cogent insights and advices at those points where the work and teaching of the former Evangelical United Brethren Church is referred to or incorporated.

Understanding The United Methodist Church is published with the hope that it may prove inspirational as well as informative and that because of it, people will want to become better United Methodists—which means better Christians.

—Nolan B. Harmon

Contents

Understanding The United Methodist Church

CHAPTER ONE

How It Started

METHODISM began in the year 1729. It began in Oxford University, England. While at college there John Wesley, Charles Wesley, George Whitefield, and a few other young men banded themselves together for the purpose of intellectual and spiritual improvement and to help one another become better Christians. So systematic were these young men in their habits of religious duty and so regular in their rules of conduct that gayer students in derision called them

METHODISTS

and the name stuck.

In like manner the disciples of Christ were first called "Christians" at Antioch by a deriding world, yet the name was appropriate, and Christians have always gloried in it. Methodism, too, has had from the first a glorious history, and none of its followers is ashamed of the name. John Wesley himself often referred to the "people called Methodists."

The Methodist movement started not with the idea of founding a church or of reforming the world, but in the earnest desire of a few young men to live better lives themselves. That was all there was to it. These young collegemates at Oxford came together to encourage one another, to pray with one another, to study God's Word with one another.

They had no idea that they were starting the vast Methodist Churches of the present—they simply longed for a closer walk with God and knew that they could help and be helped by one

9

another if they met regularly and asked God to bless them. There were a good many other small religious societies over England at that time, and the "Holy Club"—another derisive name for the group—was not extraordinary except in the youth of its members and the fact that they were students in a cold, classic university.

The First Regular Methodist Society

The first Methodist society was organized in London in 1739 by John Wesley with about ten other persons. It soon swelled to hundreds, with other societies organizing in London and the English realm. A great revival of religion began to spread over the land and in time extended throughout the world. It was a work of depth and duration, and God was in it. Today, long after those beginning days, it still goes on and will go on wherever sincere souls, by whatever name they are called, continue to seek and find the way and will of God for themselves.

The Methodist movement came, as one writer said,

sweeping along like the winds which God had let loose from his fists, swaying devout souls, breaking down stubborn sinners, overturning hopes built on false foundations, but quenching not the smoking flax, nor breaking the bruised reed. It was Heaven's bountiful gift to the silent prayer of the world's sorrow by reason of its great sin.[1]

Methodism emphasized what we call "experiential religion." Something happened that men and women *felt*. They knew for themselves that there is a God and that he forgives sins, accepts the sinner, and makes him his child. They knew this because it happened to them. Salvation, they found, was not something read of in a book, nor preached from a pulpit—it was something lived in life and known as immediate, firsthand experience. They meant it when they sang:

> O how happy are they
> Who the Saviour obey,

[1] H. T. Hudson, *The Methodist Armor.*

And have laid up their treasure above!
Tongue can never express
The sweet comfort and peace
Of a soul in its earliest love.

Every Methodist was expected to have some sort of Christian experience, something he or she could be sure of, something he or she could tell to others.

These first Methodists were not happy unless and until they were telling others of God and of what he had done for them. So the "experience meeting" came to be a feature of many early Methodist gatherings. In such meetings and elsewhere the account of those who had found God stirred others, and they in turn stirred others. The revival rolled on.

By the genius of its leader, John Wesley, and by the systematic way the societies worked and worshiped, the Methodist revival began early to express itself in definite patterns of activity. So class meetings, love feasts, conferences, came into being—also stewards, class leaders, and an itinerant ministry— that is, a moving and traveling one. A well-integrated organization—though not as yet a separate church—began to take shape as each new duty or emergency called for some action or plan to meet it.

The Methodist idea of church organization has always been that the power of the divine Spirit will express itself through whatever forms are needed to perpetuate and spread the gospel, and that the church itself must be flexible enough in its orders and processes to follow wherever the Spirit seems to lead. Every true church must be constantly making adjustments to new challenges and new situations, keeping always the solid, sure, scriptural basis of the Christian life.

Within ten years after the start of the United Societies of Methodism in England, the outlines of the future Church were becoming visible and the patterns of its organization taking shape. There was then no idea that there would be a Methodist Church, for all were loyal members of the Church of England. Societies formed in separate places, however, were tied to one another in what Methodists then and now speak of as a "connection." Quarterly meetings in each local church

11

were held, and business was transacted much as in our present Charge Conferences. Annual meetings of the preachers soon became known as the Annual Conference. A preaching ministry thus came about, with men speaking and witnessing and traveling according to a uniform system. So Methodism was off on its glorious career.

John Wesley, The Founder

Wesley was one of the most remarkable men who ever lived. He combined great energy and organizing ability with religious genius of the highest order.

He was born in Epworth parsonage in Lincolnshire, England, in 1703. His father, Samuel Wesley, was a clergyman of the Church of England; his mother, Susanna Wesley, was one of the great mothers of men. Pious, cultured, and strict, she brought up her large family of children according to exact religious rules of everyday living. The Epworth parsonage in its rigorous discipline became the cradle of Methodism. A great many Methodist rules for sincere Christian living had their origin at Epworth. To this background of a devoted home Wesley added the distinction of becoming one of the most famous graduates of Oxford University. While at Oxford he decided to become a clergyman of the Church and in due time was ordained as such. He was tremendously in earnest in his religious life, and with the other members of the Holy Club he spent his time in doing good "over and above the call of duty." He visited the jail inmates, ministered to the poor, attended Communion services regularly.

However, in all this John Wesley was not happy—he felt that there should be a joy and peace in religion which he did not have. Then he decided to go to America and help convert the Indians in the newly opened province of Georgia. Charles Wesley, his brother, had been made secretary to General Oglethorpe, who was in charge of the Georgia colony. So the Wesley brothers sailed for Savannah, where John Wesley spent some months as rector of the Savannah church. But his ministry was neither happy nor successful, and he went

12

back to England. There, still seeking to find God, he had an experience which changed his whole life.

While sitting in a prayer meeting in an Aldersgate Street house in London with a small company of Christians, he said that he felt his heart "strangely warmed." "I felt I did trust in Christ, Christ alone for salvation; and an assurance was given me that he had taken away my sins, even mine, and saved me from the law of sin and death."

From that minute John Wesley was a changed man. Before his "conversion," as we call it, he knew what religion was theoretically; afterward he knew practically—or, as we say, experientially. No longer was it what the books had said or what the church lecturers had maintained, but what he himself *knew.* And what Wesley found that God could do for him, he knew God could do for others—and he began to preach it with might and main.

From that time on John Wesley was a man full of power and of the Holy Spirit. His intellectual faculties were greatly kindled, his spiritual wisdom grew, and his energy knew no bounds. Soon he began to travel and to preach and to organize into societies, or bands, all who were converted. A vast and growing spiritual movement took place under his leadership. England soon began to ring with the Methodist revival.

Wesley did two things which greatly magnified the power and force of Methodism: (1) he created a corps of lay preachers (local preachers or lay pastors, we would call them) who gave all the time they could to preaching under his direction; (2) he adopted outdoor, or field, preaching in a big way. This was simply preaching out of doors in any convenient place—in a meadow, a vacant city lot, on the steps of a building, anywhere. In this way Wesley and his preachers took the gospel to those who otherwise never would have heard it.

Methodist preachers soon were seen going everywhere. They held their meetings wherever they could get people to listen, while men and women who had been converted backed them up by telling publicly how God had changed their lives. Crowds flocked to hear, and the revival grew apace. Singing was heard —such singing as England never had known before. Charles

13

Wesley, the brother of John, began to write hymns, as did others; and the enthusiastic chorus of outdoor multitudes awakened England, Wales, Scotland, and North Ireland. Everywhere people who had been dead to religion found happiness and purpose in life and in turn told others.

But all was not smooth sailing. The regular clergy of the Church of England, especially the bishops, frowned on all such irregular goings on. They called it "enthusiasm" and would have none of it. The Bishop of Bristol told John Wesley that he was not commissioned to preach in his diocese and had no business there. Wesley replied that his business on earth was to do what good he could and "woe is me if I preach not the gospel wherever I am in the habitable world."

To another clergyman critical on the same point Wesley gave the historic reply that Methodism has nailed to her masthead ever since: "I look upon all the world as my parish."

For some years there was active hostility to the movement and some real persecution. Mobs in several places broke up the Methodist outdoor meetings with sticks and stones. Wesley himself was stoned and mobbed several times, and one or two of his preachers were killed. But God was in the revival, and it kept spreading. Bad men became good; drunkards became sober; religion wrote itself in changed lives everywhere, and this could not be denied. Wesley lived to see Methodism established widely over the English-speaking world; and when he died, full of years and of honor, he could say sincerely, "The best of all is, God is with us."

American Methodism

Methodism, which swept through England, in time crossed the Atlantic and was destined to influence tremendously the whole American continent.

The first American society was organized in New York by Philip Embury, a local preacher. He was prompted to do this by his cousin Barbara Heck, a Christian woman who had become greatly concerned over the worldliness which seemed to be engulfing them all. Embury and Barbara Heck were emigrants from Ireland and were originally of German stock.

14

Embury had been a preacher for a time in Ireland. As the story goes, one day Barbara Heck came in and found a card game in progress. With a sudden defiant move she seized the cards, threw them into the fire, and whirled on Embury: "Philip, if you don't preach to us, we will all go to hell."

Embury, aroused in conscience because he knew that he had been neglectful, began to preach and exhort. A small society was started. A British army officer named Captain Webb, a man of some means, shortly after joined the group; and in 1768 the first Methodist chapel was built on John Street, New York. The John Street Church still stands today amid the skyscrapers of the Wall Street district. Two brass candlesticks which Dame Barbara brought to "meeting" and then took home afterward now are standing squarely on either side of the John Street pulpit—fit emblems of an indomitable woman.

At about the same time that John Street was started, an Irish emigrant named Robert Strawbridge built a Methodist log chapel at Sam's Creek in Maryland. Here began another Methodist group destined to live and grow. The John Street society consisted of but fifty persons a few years after its founding; Strawbridge's log meeting house did not have that large a following. But the power of God was with them; and "as green forests sleep in the tiny cup of acorns, so grand possibilities slumbered in this mustard seed of vital religion."

In 1769 Richard Boardman and Joseph Pilmoor, the first itinerant preachers sent by Wesley to "American circuit," arrived. Boardman was stationed at John Street in New York, Pilmoor as pastor in Philadelphia.

Two years later, in 1771, Wesley sent to America Francis Asbury, a man who was destined under God to influence and shape the growing Methodist connection in America more than any other man. Asbury was but a youth when he arrived but within a few years, and thereafter until his death in 1816, was the acknowledged and undisputed leader of the whole connection in America.

In 1773 the first Annual Conference was held at Philadelphia. There were ten preachers present—Thomas Rankin, Richard Boardman, Joseph Pilmoor, Francis Asbury, Richard Wright,

15

George Shadford, Thomas Webb, John King, A. Whitworth, Joseph Yearbry—names which remain in Methodist history as do those of the signers of the Declaration of Independence in national annals. These men looked after 6 circuits and 1,160 members.

Meanwhile Methodism spread to the South, where in Maryland and Virginia it was destined to have marvelous growth. In 1774 Robert Williams began to organize societies in Virginia, and two years later farther south the "Carolina" Circuit came into being. Williams was a rousing preacher, always on the move with the true evangelist's zeal for getting things done at once. Virginia and Carolina Methodists both can look back to Robert Williams as their spiritual father. Although the American Revolution broke with full fury on these colonies in 1777-78, even during its dark and bitter days great revivals were held in the tidewater country of Virginia and North Carolina. Eighteen hundred souls were added to these societies in one year.

But the Methodist congregations, which called themselves societies as long as the colonies belonged to England, had to become a church after America was free. For the Church of England (to which most of the Methodists looked for ordained clergymen to give them the sacraments) had, of course, gone with the withdrawal of English rule. The Methodists in the United States thereupon felt compelled, and indeed were glad, to unite into a church, which should be thereafter a self-governing, independent, Christian church, to the glory of God and the advancement of his kingdom.

Organization of the Church

The Methodist Episcopal Church was formally organized at a conference of Methodist ministers in Baltimore in the last week of December, 1784. Famous in Methodist annals as the Christmas Conference (as it began December 25 and lasted until January 2, 1785), this organization meeting put its stamp upon all subsequent actions and the entire future development of Methodism in America.

16

It adopted a name, The Methodist Episcopal Church. This indicated that the church should be Methodist in its doctrine and discipline, and Episcopal, that is, organized under bishops, in its form of church government.

The Christmas Conference also adopted a prayer book known as the *Sunday Service*, sent over by John Wesley. This contained the Articles of Religion, which the present church still holds, and also directed the manner of conducting worship, especially in the sacramental services, marriage, burial, and so on. As the *Sunday Service* was an abridgment of the *Book of Common Prayer* of the Church of England, this accounts for the similarity between our Methodist worship and ritual and that of the Church of England and also that of the Episcopal Church in America.

The Christmas Conference also elected two men as bishops for the Methodist Episcopal Church—Francis Asbury and Thomas Coke. These, the first Methodist bishops, were at first called superintendents; but in a few years the title was changed to Bishop.

Twelve other men were elected "elders" by the Christmas Conference, ordained to be ministers and empowered to administer communion. Up to that time Methodist preachers had been simply "preachers" and had no right to administer the sacraments. They were viewed as laymen who went about preaching in a sort of irregular way. But at the Christmas Conference and afterward men were ordained into the ministry of the Methodist Episcopal Church; and their orders—that is, their ministerial status—were never questioned by any except a few high-church persons who felt that no one could be rightly ordained except by an English bishop. Today the validity of Methodist orders is generally recognized over the entire church world.

It is necessary to describe rather fully the Christmas Conference of 1784, for in importance it outranks all subsequent general church gatherings. While Methodism had its roots deep in the established Church of England and in the historic church of the past, and while it can claim an unbroken chain of ordinations and of churchly practice reaching far back, the

Christmas Conference truly gave to the world a new church. That church was destined to increase and multiply at first by tens of thousands, then by hundred of thousands, and now by millions; and, please God, it shall continue so long as it can and will carry out the will of God.

An old history of New Jersey, when surveying the religious life of that state, says rather dryly: "The Methodists got started about the time of the Revolution, but after it, for the next fifty years, Methodism like a great wave rolled over Jersey." It rolled over all the colonies, then over the states, then across the passes in the Appalachians to the Mississippi, the western plains, and on to the shores of the Pacific. Growth was marvelous. By 1796 there were 56,664 members; by 1806, 130,570; in 1826, 360,800; in 1836, 650,103; at the time of the Civil War 1,032,184.[2] That war interrupted life greatly, especially in the South; and Methodism lost thousands, but in a few years regained its power and went ahead. Annual Conference after Annual Conference was organized as the church grew and as the American people themselves multiplied.

The Methodist Church was peculiarly suited to the American scene, whether it was the frontier or the crowded city; it is suited to the American temperament, which it has always expressed and embodied in all its actions and viewpoints. Both preachers and people have been part and parcel of the nation itself. The big Methodist faults—and we have them, let us confess—are the big American faults; and the big Methodist virtues—and, thank God, we have them, too—are the big American virtues. Our church is in fact not only the largest but the most evenly distributed Protestant church in the United States. When Theodore Roosevelt was President, he once privately remarked to the chaplain of the United States Senate, who was a Methodist, "Your church is the church of America."

Alongside the great growth in numbers went a vast development in all other areas of church life. Missions to foreign lands as well as those at home were started early in the nineteenth

---

[2] Abel Stevens, A *Compendious History of American Methodism.*

18

century. Melville Cox, the first native American missionary, went to Africa; other brave pioneers to India. Soon the spreading sails of moving ships were taking men and women from our shores to the ends of the earth, while the home churches supported them with money and with prayers. Stories began to come back—stories of success almost apostolic—together with insistent calls for more men and more money. Liberally the home conferences responded until the far-flung empire of Methodist missions was flying its flag over fifty-five nations of the earth.

Schools and colleges were built, keeping pace with the growth of the church. Beginning with Cokesbury College at Abingdon, Maryland, other institutions were added—academies, seminaries, colleges, universities—until today the Church has under its charge or directly related to it many nationally known institutions of higher learning and all kinds of secondary schools, training centers, and the like.

Orphanages and homes for the needy, the aged, and the infirm were soon erected by the growing church. To take care of the fatherless and the widows and to help the sick and the afflicted has always been a Christian goal. Methodism is proud of the assertion once made regarding it, that it is "Christianity in earnest."

Time would fail to tell of the other great works of the United Methodist Church, though some of these will be referred to later in this book. Enough has been said to indicate that the church grew not only in numbers but in its effective outreach to mankind. The United Methodist *Discipline* truly states: "The United Methodist Church believes today as Methodism has from the first, that the only infallible proof of a true church of Christ is its ability to seek and save the lost, to disseminate the Pentecostal spirit and life, to spread scriptural holiness and to transform all peoples and nations through the gospel of Christ." Toward the fulfilling of this ideal purpose The United Methodist Church has not been behind in any generation.

In its growth the Methodist Church in the United States was divided a number of times. Two divisions were of high importance. One was the withdrawal in 1828 of Methodists who called for greater lay rights in the church. These subsequently organized the Methodist Protestant Church. This church had a long and honored history, and its members lived to see the Methodist Episcopal Churches adopt the principle of lay representation which the original Methodist Protestants had withdrawn to secure. The Methodist Protestants joined in the great move for Methodist union in 1939 and played a big part in consummating it.

In 1844 the original Methodist Episcopal Church divided, and the Methodist Episcopal Church, South, was organized. The reasons for this epochal separation were variously interpreted by representatives of the two sections. Northern Methodists claimed it was due to the South's holding onto slavery. Southern Methodists claimed it was over the question as to the power of the General Conference over a bishop. A vast sectional cleavage was behind the division, and the Civil War soon proved how far apart men in the same church might be when it came to social and political questions. Happily, after the long years had healed the hurt of war and allayed the fierce antagonisms of earlier days, the two churches came together in an unbreakable union in 1939 and with the Methodist Protestant Church formed THE METHODIST CHURCH.

The Evangelical United Brethren

Meanwhile growing in parallel with American Methodism were two other bodies of Christians destined in time to unite first with each other, and then with The Methodist Church. These two bodies began in the early part of the nineteenth century and at their very beginning had close connections with the new and growing Methodist Episcopal Church. One of these was the Church of the United Brethren in Christ; the other was the Evangelical Church, which was the result of the union of the Evangelical Association and the United Evangelical Church.

Philip William Otterbein, an ordained minister of the German Reformed Church, and Martin Boehm, a Pennsylvanian

20

of Mennonite parentage, are given credit for founding the United Brethren in Christ. Otterbein was a friend of Francis Asbury and, at Asbury's request, assisted Dr. Coke in the ordination of Asbury at the Christmas Conference. Otterbein and Boehm led a spiritual revival among the German-speaking settlers of the middle colonies. Some have insisted that the United Brethren in Christ were simply German-speaking Methodists, and in fact their organization as it formally developed adopted much of the pattern of the Methodist Episcopal Church. It also reinforced and was reinforced by the evangelistic spirit which marked Methodism. Meetings of ministerial groups of the United Brethren in Christ were held annually beginning in 1800. Martin Boehm died in 1812, and Otterbein who by that time was incapacitated by illness, asked that Christian Newcomer, another pioneer leader, should be elected as superintendent (or bishop) in 1813 to oversee and direct the work of the growing church.

The Church of the United Brethren in Christ increased greatly, as did Methodism, through outward expansion. Newcomer engaged in fellowship with the Methodists and hoped to bring about a closer union, but the difficulties proved too great.

The first General Conference in what came to be called the United Brethren in Christ was held June 6, 1815, and a *Book of Discipline* was authorized. The book together with a constitution adopted in 1841 provided regulations under which the United Brethren Church—as it was often called—expanded in numbers and mission.

A serious division came about in the Church of the United Brethren in 1889 due to changes made in the constitution of that church by a majority of the General Conference. The leader of the minority group was Bishop Milton Wright, the father of Wilbur and Orville Wright, the airplane pioneers. The United Brethren Church brought its large connection into union with the Evangelical Church in 1946 to form the Evangelical United Brethren Church. Then in 1968 this body united with The Methodist Church to constitute The United Methodist Church.

21

The Evangelical Association

Jacob Albright, a godly minister of Pennsylvania, who was first a Lutheran then a Methodist, is looked upon as the founder of the Evangelical Association, as it was first called. In 1800 he began instructing small groups of German-speaking persons in Pennsylvania who desired to be "saved from their sins and flee from the wrath to come"—the exact language John Wesley employed in explaining how he came to give the General Rules. Albright formed several "classes," and in November, 1803, the first council of this group was held. All happened to be Pennsylvanians.

The first conference of the group was held in 1807 at what is now Kleinfeltersville, Pennsylvania. For a time they took the name, "The Newly Formed Methodist Conference." Sometimes they were spoken of as the "German Methodist Church." They continued to meet and grow, and in 1816 at the first General Conference of the body, the name "The Evangelical Association" was adopted. This church grew but in 1892 divided over what has been called "an unfortunate misunderstanding." By 1910 the growing conviction that the two divided churches should be reunited found expression, and in 1922 the Evangelical Association and the United Evangelical Church united under the name The Evangelical Church. In 1946 the Evangelical Church united with the Church of the United Brethren in Christ to form the Evangelical United Brethren Church. The growth of the United Brethren and of the Evangelical Church connection, like that of the Methodist churches everywhere, was marked by intense missionary activity, the creation of strong educational institutions, forthright church publications, a well wrought Sunday school literature, and the comprehensive activity of a modern Christian church. Negotiations looking toward the union of the E.U.B. with The Methodist Church were carried on for several years before actual union came about in Dallas, Texas, in 1968. The body there formed took the name **The United Methodist Church.** That body vast in numbers and influence, continues to write its own history.

CHAPTER TWO

Doctrine and Beliefs

The United Methodist Church is a Christian church standing squarely on the Bible for its doctrine and belief. It is a Protestant church. It holds to the essentials of pure Christianity as reemphasized in the Protestant Reformation when Martin Luther and other Protestant reformers broke with the Church of Rome in the sixteenth century.

Methodist beliefs are embodied and expressed in a terse, concrete way in the Apostles' Creed. "Methodism is settled in the apostolic theology," said Bishop Horace M. DuBose in *The Symbol of Methodism*. "The Apostles' Creed . . . is its Creed." This creed, or affirmation of faith, United Methodists are expected to repeat Sunday after Sunday as part of their worship. United Methodist standards of doctrine are more definitely stated in

TWENTY-FIVE ARTICLES OF RELIGION
THE CONFESSION OF FAITH
FIFTY-TWO SERMONS OF JOHN WESLEY, AND
NOTES ON THE NEW TESTAMENT BY JOHN WESLEY

The Articles accompanied by the Confession of Faith, the Sermons, and the Notes are commonly taken as the United Methodist standards of doctrine. But as the fifty-two sermons (which Wesley selected as containing the doctrines he held) and his *Notes on the New Testament* are difficult to boil down, American Methodists have usually taken the Articles of

23

Religion as the concrete expression of their belief. Where there may be a question as to the meaning of an Article or its specific interpretation, they refer back to the preaching or teaching of Wesley and the early Methodist preachers to settle the matter.

The Confession of Faith was the formal doctrinal affirmation of the Evangelical United Brethren Church before its union with The Methodist Church. At that union the Confession was formally adopted as a standard of doctrine of the United Methodist Church and is published in the *Discipline* of the Church as "constitutional matter," as are the Articles of Religion. Its sixteen divisions ("articles") largely parallel many of the historic Methodist Articles of Religion, and we will show them in connection with their kindred Articles in the next few pages.

Methodists have never been too doctrinally conscious. They "lead with their hearts instead of their heads," [1] a popular magazine once said of them. The practical living of the Christian life has always meant more to Methodists than hairsplitting theological discussions. "Is thine heart right as my heart is with thy heart?" Wesley was accustomed to ask when men wanted to argue with him over matters of doctrine. "If it is, give me thy hand." Another time he explained, "In opinions that do not strike at the root of Christianity, we Methodists think and let think."

To help present day church members understand their faith in the kind of world in which we live, the 1972 General Conference of The United Methodist Church adopted a set of guide lines for the interpretation of Christian beliefs. These guide lines in no way replace the Articles and the Confession of Faith but state how these are to be understood. These guide lines to such understanding are:

SCRIPTURE, first—for all must be based upon that;
CHRISTIAN TRADITION, or what Christians who have lived before us have taught us regarding their Faith as that was based on Scripture and lived in life;

[1] *Newsweek*, May 10, 1948, "Methodists: Stock Taking."

24

EXPERIENCE, or one's own personal appreciation and ap-
propriation of God's message and meaning in one's spiritual life;

REASON, or using our mental powers and the mind God
has given us to understand and think through the truths
of our faith.

"These four are interdependent" said the statement
adopted by the General Conference; "None can be defined
unambiguously." All are to be relied on together. Reason and
experience must check and be checked by Scripture, and all
the teaching of the Christian past as the church has passed
this down to us must be listened to if we are to follow "in the
way our fathers trod."

The Bishops of The Methodist Church addressing the General Conference of 1952 said: "Our theology has never been
a closely organized doctrinal system. We have never insisted
on uniformity of thought or statement." But—they went
on—"There are great Christian doctrines which we most surely hold and firmly believe." Methodists have always heatedly
rejected the idea that Methodism is simply a "movement"
with no formal doctrine. The Bishops in the address above
cited went on to emphasize this idea. "There are great Christian doctrines which we most surely hold and firmly believe."

We now take up the Articles of Religion and their parallel
statements in the Confession of Faith. The Articles were
taken from the Thirty-nine Articles of the Church of England
by John Wesley and sent to American Methodism after
Wesley had carefully abridged and edited them. The Methodist Church in America adopted them as setting forth its
faith, and The United Methodist Church holds them to be
part of the constitution of the church.

No United Methodist or group of United Methodists, not
even the General Conference of the Church, has a right to
change the articles even by one word. These historic statements of our faith can only be altered by a long, drawn-out
process of amending the constitution. This requires four years

to effect and the all but unanimous consent of the whole church acting together.

In the succeeding pages we publish the Articles of Religion and the Confession of Faith in order. We will show how they are each based on biblical truth and then will try to make clear in modern language their underlying meaning. The interpretation given will be as nearly as possible that of John Wesley and the Methodist theologians up to and through the nineteenth century. The guide lines of Scripture, Tradition, Experience, and Reason, as approved by the 1972 General Conference are to be brought to bear upon each interpretation.

It is important to realize that almost every one of these articles was written in answer to a direct question or direct challenge to some point of faith. Certain articles, for instance, were to answer infidels or agnostics who wanted to know what the Church believed about God and Christ. Some were to refute Roman Catholic teachings about the sacraments or worship of saints; some were to answer Calvinists and their teachings. The fact that the articles came about to answer special challenges explains why they do not cover *everything* a Christian may believe.

It will also explain the ancient phraseology of the articles. Some of them spend time on issues no longer alive and of no great interest to modern Christians. The Confession of Faith, it will be seen, is much more modern in its language than are the articles. Nevertheless both Articles and Confession do set forth, if in a somewhat stilted way, the main tenets of the Christian faith as The United Methodist Church officially holds them.

The Articles of Religion and the separate divisions of the Confession of Faith which go with them are as follows:

1. Of Faith in the Holy Trinity

There is but one living and true God, everlasting, without body or parts, of infinite power, wisdom, and goodness; the maker and preserver of all things, visible and invisible. And in the unity of this Godhead there are

three persons, of one substance, power and eternity—
the Father, the Son and the Holy Ghost.

(Confession) Article I—God

We believe in the one true, holy and living God,
Eternal Spirit, who is Creator, Sovereign and Preserver
of all things visible and invisible. He is infinite in power,
wisdom, goodness and love, and rules with gracious regard for the well-being and salvation of men, to the glory
of his name. We believe the one God reveals himself as
the Trinity: Father, Son and Holy Spirit, distinct but in-
separable, eternally one in essence and power.

Scriptural Basis: [3] "Hear, O Israel: the Lord our God is one Lord."
(Deut. 6:4) "Thou, even thou, art Lord alone; thou hast made
heaven, the heaven of heavens, with all their host, the earth, and
all things that are therein, the seas, and all that is therein, and thou
preservest them all." (Neh. 9:6.) "Holy, holy, holy, is the Lord of
hosts: the whole earth is full of his glory." (Isa. 6:3.) "But the
Lord is the true God, he is the living God." (Jer. 10:10.) "From
everlasting to everlasting, thou art God." (Ps. 90:2.) "One God
and Father of all." (Eph. 4:6.) "God is a Spirit." (John 4:24.)
"God is love." (I John 4:16.) "To God only wise, be glory."
(Rom. 16:27.) "Now unto the King eternal, immortal, invisible,
the only wise God, be honour and glory for ever and ever. Amen."
(I Tim. 1:17.)

This, the first of all affirmations of faith, asserts belief in
God—God as creator, God as all-powerful, and God as good.
All who are not atheists (who do not believe in any god) or
agnostics (who say they don't know) can join with us in
agreeing to the first part of this article. Jews and Moslems, as
well as Christians of all sects, agree about the greatness and
power and watch care of God.

God is *one*—so true faith has always insisted against all
people, ancient or modern, who worship many gods. That

[3] The scriptural basis cited in connection with this and other articles
is not to be thought of as a resort to prooftexts. Rather since scripture
is the chief guideline for all faith, we give here the particular affirmations
which highlight and emphasize the broader truths which the Church has
always steadfastly believed.

God is a *living* God is asserted against all idol worshipers or those who think God to be a vast cosmic principle that, they suppose, runs the world. Our God is a living Person, whether called Jehovah or Lord or whatever name.

Notice the attributes or characteristics of God. He is *everlasting;* he is *without body or parts*—that is, he is not like the things or people he has created. He is far greater. Also he is a *Spirit*, as Jesus told the Samaritan woman (John 4:24). He is infinite in *power*, in *wisdom*, and in *goodness*.

God is good, and God is great—these are the two attributes of God on which Christianity bases its whole theology and on which we rest our complete hope. Even when we pass through the valley of the shadow of death, we fear no evil, resting in the goodness and greatness of God. " '*Infinite* goodness!' " exclaimed a Methodist bishop years ago; " 'the glorious gospel of the blessed God' [is] wrapped up in that matchless phrase." [4]

2. Of the Word, or Son of God, Who Was Made Very Man

The Son, who is the Word of the Father, the very and eternal God, of one substance with the Father, took man's nature in the womb of the blessed Virgin; so that two whole and perfect natures, that is to say, the Godhead and Manhood, were joined together in one person, never to be divided; whereof is one Christ, very God and very Man, who truly suffered, was crucified, dead, and buried, to reconcile his Father to us, and to be a sacrifice, not only for original guilt, but also for the actual sins of men.

(Confession) Article II—Jesus Christ

We believe in Jesus Christ, truly God and truly man, in whom the divine and human natures are perfectly and inseparably united. He is the eternal Word made flesh, the only begotten Son of the Father, born of the Virgin

[4] H. M. DuBose, *The Symbol of Methodism.*

28

Mary by the power of the Holy Spirit. As ministering Servant he lived, suffered and died on the cross. He was buried, rose from the dead, and ascended into heaven to be with the Father, from whence he shall return. He is eternal Savior and Mediator, who intercedes for us, and by him all men will be judged.

SCRIPTURAL BASIS: "There is one God, and one mediator between God and men, the man Christ Jesus." (I Tim. 2:5.) "But to us there is but one God, the Father, of whom are all things, and we in him; and one Lord Jesus Christ, by whom are all things, and we by him." (I Cor. 8:6.) "In the beginning was the Word, and the Word was with God and the Word was God." (John 1:1.) "The Word was made flesh, and dwelt among us, (and we beheld his glory, the glory as of the only begotten of the Father,) full of grace and truth." (John 1:14.) "In him dwelleth all the fulness of the Godhead bodily." (Col. 2:9.) "I came forth from the Father, and am come into the world: again, I leave the world, and go to the Father." (John 16:28.) "He that hath seen me hath seen the Father." (John 14:9.) "God, having raised up his Son Jesus, sent him to bless you, in turning away every one of you from his iniquities." (Acts 3:26.) "Thou art that Christ, the Son of the living God." (John 6:69.)

This is the first distinctively Christian affirmation of faith. This article sets forth in one long sentence the whole matter of the gospel: that God became man and lived on earth; that Godhood and manhood were joined together in one person, Jesus Christ, who was truly both God and man; and that this Christ was "crucified, dead, and buried" to restore the broken fellowship of God and man, and save men from their sins. This is the gospel. This is the good news. How, or in what manner, Christ effected this is something else; but that it has been done is as clear as sunlight—Christ is our redeemer.

Jews and Moslems believe in God, but Christians believe in Jesus Christ as the divine Son of God. "These are written," John explains as he finishes his whole Gospel, "that ye might believe that Jesus [whose life and deeds he sets forth] *is the Christ*, . . . and that believing ye might have life through his name." (20:31.) Christianity is Christ.

29

3. Of the Resurrection of Christ

Christ did truly rise again from the dead, and took again his body, with all things appertaining to the perfection of man's nature, wherewith he ascended into heaven, and there sitteth until he return to judge all men at the last day.

(Confession) Article XII—The Judgment and the Future State

We believe all men stand under the righteous judgment of Jesus Christ, both now and in the last day. We believe in the resurrection of the dead; the righteous to life eternal and the wicked to endless condemnation.

SCRIPTURAL BASIS: All the Gospels tell of the Resurrection in detail. "Go quickly and tell his disciples that he is risen from the dead." (Matt. 28:7.) "But now is Christ risen from the dead, and become the firstfruits of them that slept." (I Cor. 15:20.)

Ascension and Session: "While they beheld, he was taken up; and a cloud received him." (Acts 1:9.) "This same Jesus, which is taken up from you into heaven, shall so come in like manner as ye have seen him go into heaven." (Acts 1:11.) "So then after the Lord had spoken unto them, he was received up into heaven, and sat on the right hand of God." (Mark 16:19.) "It is Christ that died, yea rather, that is risen again, who is even at the right hand of God, who also maketh intercession for us." (Rom. 8:34.) "When [God] raised him from the dead, and set him at his own right hand in the heavenly places." (Eph. 1:20.) "This man, after he had offered one sacrifice for sins for ever, sat down on the right hand of God." (Heb. 10:12.)

Second Advent and Judgment: "If I go and prepare a place for you, I will come again, and receive you unto myself." (John 14:3) "Our conversation is in heaven; from whence also we look for the Saviour, the Lord Jesus Christ." (Phil. 3:20.) "Whom the heavens must receive until the times of restitution of all things." (Acts 3:21.) "When the Lord Jesus shall be revealed from heaven with his mighty angels." (II

Thess. 1:7.) "[God] hath appointed a day, in which he will judge the world in righteousness by that man whom he hath ordained; whereof he hath given assurance unto all men, in that he hath raised him from the dead." (Acts 17:31.) "For the Father judgeth no man, but hath committed all judgment unto the Son." (John 5:22.)

The resurrection of Christ, as affirmed in Article 3, was the seal and confirmation of all Jesus' teachings, of all that he had said of himself. When Christ rose from the dead, he not only certified to the truth of all that had been believed regarding him, but started a new order of beings in the universe of God. He was, as the apostle Paul said, the "firstfruits of them that slept." That is, by being the first to rise among all those who had died since time began, he assumed first place in the new order of God.

Christianity may yield on other points, but it cannot yield on the Resurrection. Our hope and our faith are based on it. There was no pretense, no lively imagination, no purely ethereal appearance. "*Five* times he showed himself alive" on the day of his resurrection—"to Mary Magdalene, to another company of women, to Peter, to two disciples on their way to Emmaus, to the eleven; to St. Thomas in the prayer-meeting; then in Galilee; to seven, and to five hundred. They knew him by many infallible proofs." [5]

Christianity is the religion of a great hope. Christ's was the first of all the graves that shall finally be opened when he shall have "put all enemies under his feet."

The last affirmation of this article has to do with the ascension of Christ, his session, and his second coming to judge the earth. The account of the Ascension and promise that the Lord shall come again is found in the first chapter of the Acts of the Apostles. The Ascension marked the end of the earthly life of Jesus but in no way ended the spiritual presence of the living Christ. He is our eternal contemporary, known to all who truly live in him.

The Session, or sitting of Christ at the right hand of God,

---

[5] Hudson, *op. cit.*

is a symbolic way of representing the fact that all power belongs to Christ both in heaven and on earth.

The final return of Christ to judge the quick and the dead—the Second Coming or Second Advent—is affirmed in this article and in the Confession, as it is in the Apostles' Creed. An eager expectation of the Lord's return is reflected at many places in the New Testament. But neither this article nor the creed undertakes to tell *when* the Lord shall return, and he himself said that he did not know (Mark 13:32). Because of the vagaries and wild prophecies of Adventist groups, and controversies between premillennialists and postmillennialists, many present-day Christians have a tendency to ignore, and some to rebel against, the whole idea of a Second Advent. Practical Christians, including most Methodists, usually take the position that since we cannot know and are not meant to know about "times and seasons," we should get on with our own daily lives and leave the rest to God. But it is undeniable that the New Testament does teach that the Lord shall return in God's own time, and this to many thoughtful Christians is the

> One far-off divine event,
> To which the whole creation moves.

4. Of the Holy Ghost

The Holy Ghost, proceeding from the Father and the Son, is of one substance, majesty, and glory, with the Father and the Son, very and eternal God.

(Confession) Article III—The Holy Spirit

We believe in the Holy Spirit who proceeds from and is one in being with the Father and the Son. He convinces the world of sin, of righteousness and of judgment. He leads men through faithful response to the gospel into the fellowship of the Church. He comforts, sustains, and empowers the faithful, and guides them into all truth.

SCRIPTURAL BASIS: "Baptizing them in the name of the Father, and of the Son, and of the Holy Ghost." (Matt. 28:19.) "When he, the Spirit of truth, is come, he will guide you into all truth." (John 16:13.) "The Spirit itself beareth witness with our spirit, that we are the children of God." (Rom. 8:16.) "Holy men of God spake as they were moved by the Holy Ghost." (II Pet. 1:21.) "And they were all filled with the Holy Ghost." (Acts 2:4.) "The Lord is that Spirit." (II Cor. 3:17.)

Our faith teaches that there is one God, but that he exists in three persons—God the Father, God the Son, and God the Holy Spirit. The Father is not the Son, nor the Holy Spirit, but is God. The Son is not the Father and not the Holy Spirit, but is God. The Holy Spirit is not the Father and not the Son, but is God. And this triune God, or God in three persons, is a "blessed Trinity," as a familiar hymn expresses it. "God Himself is the Father revealed; God Himself is in Christ revealing; God Himself is the Holy Spirit abiding."

The human mind cannot fathom the exact relationship of God within himself, and for ages men have asked how three can be one and not three. But to all this the heart has an answer which words can never completely express: whoever knows God, feels his Spirit, and loves his Son is at peace in the Father's keeping.

The coming of the Holy Ghost, or the divine Comforter, at Pentecost marked the definite beginning of the new Dispensation. (Acts 2:4.) Pentecost was the name of a Jewish festival day, fifty days after the Passover. But in the Christian calendar it became the birthday of the Church.

Before that day came, the small band of disciples were timid and afraid. They met secretly behind closed doors "for fear of the Jews." They seemed to be waiting for something; as indeed they were, for they had been promised "power from on high." That power was given on the day of Pentecost when the Holy Spirit came upon the disciples. Immediately everything changed. No more were there secret meetings in closed upper rooms. The lambs had become lions, and Peter stood out on the street and preached with tremendous courage and boldness. The Holy Spirit had come to be with God's own forever.

That Spirit still continues to lead and guide and will always direct the people who are his. Belief in the Holy Spirit is belief not in the dead past but in the living present and the glorious future, for he continues to show us "things to come." William F. Warren's great hymn puts it:

> I worship Thee, O Holy Ghost,
> I love to worship Thee;
> With Thee each day is Pentecost,
> Each night Nativity.

5. Of the Sufficiency of the Holy Scriptures for Salvation

The Holy Scriptures contain all things necessary to salvation; so that whatsoever is not read therein, nor may be proved thereby, is not to be required of any man that it should be believed as an article of faith, or be thought requisite or necessary to salvation. In the name of the Holy Scriptures we do understand those canonical books of the Old and New Testament of whose authority was never any doubt in the Church. The names of the canonical books are:

Genesis, Exodus, Leviticus, Numbers, Deuteronomy, Joshua, Judges, Ruth, The First Book of Samuel, The Second Book of Samuel, The First Book of Kings, The Second Book of Kings, The First Book of Chronicles, The Second Book of Chronicles, The Book of Ezra, The Book of Nehemiah, The Book of Esther, The Book of Job, The Psalms, The Proverbs, Ecclesiastes or the Preacher, Cantica or Song of Solomon, Four Prophets the Greater, Twelve Prophets the Less.

All the books of the New Testament, as they are commonly received, we do receive and account canonical.

(Confession) Article IV—The Holy Bible

We believe the Holy Bible, Old and New Testaments, reveals the Word of God so far as it is necessary for our salvation. It is to be received through the Holy Spirit as the true rule and guide for faith and practice. Whatever is not revealed in or established by the Holy Scriptures is not to be made an article of faith nor is it to be taught as essential to salvation.

SCRIPTURAL BASIS: "The law of the Lord is perfect, converting the soul: the testimony of the Lord is sure, making wise the simple." (Ps. 19:7.) "Search the scriptures; for in them ye think ye have eternal life: and they are they which testify of me." (John 5:39.) "From a child thou hast known the holy scriptures, which are able to make thee wise unto salvation." (II Tim. 3:15.) "And receive with meekness the engrafted word, which is able to save your souls." (Jas. 1:21.) "And beginning at Moses and all the prophets, he [Jesus] expounded unto them in all the scriptures the things concerning himself." (Luke 24:27.)

The first sentence of the article above is the bedrock of Protestantism. The Bible contains *all things necessary to salvation*. That is the prime affirmation. The Bible contains all sorts of other things also, let us admit—history, philosophy, poetry, wisdom, law; and a reverent scholarship can help greatly in understanding and explaining all these. But through all the study of expositors and interpreters, believers or unbelievers, the Bible stands exactly where this article of our faith says it does, as the one writing containing all things needful to a person's salvation. As salvation depends upon Christ, so Christians believe that the purpose of all scripture from Genesis to the final word in Revelation is to lead us to Christ. As Mary Lathbury's hymn puts it:

> Beyond the sacred page
> I seek Thee, Lord;
> My spirit pants for Thee,
> O living Word!

Further, whatsoever is not read in the Bible or cannot be proved by it is not to be required of any man as something to be believed. This part of the article properly asserts that the traditions of men and of the Church itself may not stand as equal to Scripture, and may not stand at all if they be contrary to Scripture. While our church in its guide lines holds tradition as of value in helping to *interpret* Scripture, no

35

Protestant church would ever assent to the pronouncement of The Council of Trent of the Roman Catholic Church that churchly traditions, written and unwritten, should be *of equal authority with the Bible,* and that "he that denies it shall be accursed." United Methodism with all Protestantism denies this flatly. If it is not in the Bible it does not have to be believed.

6. Of the Old Testament

The Old Testament is not contrary to the New; for both in the Old and New Testament everlasting life is offered to mankind by Christ, who is the only Mediator between God and man, being both God and Man. Wherefore they are not to be heard who feign that the old fathers did look only for transitory promises. Although the law given from God by Moses as touching ceremonies and rites doth not bind Christians, nor ought the civil precepts thereof of necessity be received in any commonwealth; yet notwithstanding, no Christian whatsoever is free from the obedience of the commandments which are called moral.

SCRIPTURAL BASIS: "Beginning at Moses and all the prophets, he expounded unto them in all the scriptures the things concerning himself. . . . And he said unto them, These are the words which I spake unto you, while I was yet with you, that all things must be fulfilled, which were written in the law of Moses, and in the prophets, and in the psalms, concerning me." (Luke 24:27, 44.) "Think not that I am come to destroy the law, or the prophets: I am not come to destroy, but to fulfil." (Matt. 5:17.)

The Old Testament is not contrary to the New. The whole Bible is here treated as a unified revelation. We are Christians, but we are heirs also of all God's promises. God, who spoke by the prophets (the Old Testament), finally spoke by his Son (the New Testament). It is a mistake, as this article teaches, to discount what the Old Testament promises. Christ himself is said to have made ninety quotations from the Old Testament to support his teachings. When tempted of the devil, his great weapon was, *"It is written."* The prophets and seers were forerunners for us. "In the Old Testament the New lies hidden: in the New, the Old stands revealed."

The Church of Christ cannot afford to forget these truths. Nevertheless, as this article affirms, Christians are not bound by all the minute regulations, the rites and ceremonies, of the law as given by Moses. Christ did away with the ceremonial law; and his people are saved by faith, not by works. But we do admit that the "commandments which are called moral," as the last line of this article insists, are binding upon all Christians.

What are the moral commandments? They are taken to comprise the Ten Commandments, as well as the deep natural principles written in the hearts of honest and just people everywhere. Even the heathen, as Paul expressed it, "do by nature the things contained in the law" (Rom. 2:14).

7. Of Original or Birth Sin

Original sin standeth not in the following of Adam (as the Pelagians do vainly talk), but it is the corruption of the nature of every man, that naturally is engendered of the offspring of Adam, whereby man is very far gone from original righteousness, and of his own nature inclined to evil, and that continually.

SCRIPTURAL BASIS: "By one man sin entered into the world, and death by sin; and so death passed upon all men, for that all have sinned." (Rom. 5:12.) "By one man's disobedience many were made sinners." (Rom. 5:19.)

The medieval church, the Puritans, and certain others have insisted that every child is "conceived and born in sin." Nothing can be further from the whole drift and drive of the religion of Jesus. "Suffer the little children to come unto me, and forbid them not: for of such is the kingdom of God" (Mark 10:14). And again, "Except ye . . . become as little children, ye shall not enter into the kingdom of heaven" (Matt. 18:3). Marriage is a holy estate; and each newborn babe comes fresh-minted, as it were, from the hand of God, bearing the impress and image of the Creator. But—and here

37

is the practical truth that was in the mind of those who wrote this article—in time everyone, no matter how pure at birth, finds within himself a powerful bent toward evil. "Of his own nature *inclined* to evil, and that continually," the article puts it.

This is sadly true. No matter how it got into man, a moral pull downward is always present. Why is this—the "corruption . . . that naturally is engendered of the offspring of Adam, whereby man is very far gone from original righteousness"? Certainly it is something that all men seem to have unfailingly inherited.

Leaving aside all theory, what we know from universal experience is that "all have sinned, and come short of the glory of God," and all do need a Savior. The way out—salvation—is not to "do what comes naturally," but to control and discipline both acts and thoughts that these may be turned upward toward God.

Education and the constant, unremitting teaching of the home, the school, and the Church help. Yet with all this something more is needed. "Ye must be born again," said Jesus. And you *must*. For just as there is a physical birth by which all are born into the world, so there is a spiritual birth—whether in a moment or through years, whether conscious or unconscious—by which men and women are born within the spiritual kingdom.

"You cannot trust human nature," is often said. It would be more accurate to say you cannot trust *unredeemed* human nature. For human nature that is redeemed and reflects on earth the Christian virtues of love, peace, joy, long-suffering, temperance, meekness, forbearance—the angels cannot surpass *that*. Temptation will be present as long as we live, but Christ can "take away our bent to sinning" and in place of the downward pull implant in us the upward leading of the divine Spirit.

8. Of Free Will

The condition of man after the fall of Adam is such that he cannot turn and prepare himself, by his own natural strength and works, to faith, and calling upon God; wherefore we have no power to do good works, pleasant and acceptable to God, without the grace of God by Christ preventing us, that we may have a good will, and working with us, when we have that good will.

(Confession) Article VII—Sin and Free Will

We believe man is fallen from righteousness and, apart from the grace of our Lord Jesus Christ, is destitute of holiness and inclined to evil. Unless a man be born again, he cannot see the Kingdom of God. In his own strength, without divine grace, man cannot do good works pleasing and acceptable to God. We believe, however, man influenced and empowered by the Holy Spirit is responsible in freedom to exercise his will for good.

SCRIPTURAL BASIS: "I am the vine, ye are the branches: He that abideth in me, and I in him, the same bringeth forth much fruit: for without me ye can do nothing." (John 15:5.) "For when we were yet without strength, in due time Christ died for the ungodly." (Rom. 5:6:) "You hath he quickened, who were dead in trespasses and sins." (Eph. 2:1.) "For it is God which worketh in you both to will and to do of his good pleasure." (Phil. 2:13.)

This statement has to do with man's power to find God, or to work his way into a right position with God, *by himself*. This article holds that no man can ever do this *unless* the grace of Christ shall "go ahead of him" (as "prevent" here means). "Prevenient grace" is the technical name given here.

In other words the gist of this article, its practical value for us today, is that we can't find God unless he first finds us. Man cannot storm the gates of heaven or break in by his own might; he must wait and pray and strive, and so let God find him—as God always does find the sincere seeker. "I would not now be seeking Thee, if I had not already been found of Thee," Pascal beautifully expressed it.

The last half of this article opens up the question: Can a bad man do any good at all? Can a non-Christian perform an

39

act pleasing to God? This article taken literally seems to say "no," but not all Christians are this positive. For one thing no one can be sure exactly how God will measure the acts of individual men; also there is a sense in which a good deed, like a gold coin, stands clear in its own right having an inherent value of its own. "It can't be wrong to do right," Robertson of Brighton once said.

Conceivably the grace of God can work in those who have never heard of the gospel. Our Lord taught that there are many who will "come from the east and west" to the judgment of God. That is, there will be unknown pagans who will take their places in God's kingdom because they have done justly and loved mercy. Good deeds alone, all admit, do not suffice; but good deeds are acceptable and pleasing in their own degree.

9. Of the Justification of Man

We are accounted righteous before God only for the merit of our Lord and Savior Jesus Christ, by faith. and not for our own works or deservings. Wherefore, that we are justified by faith only is a most wholesome doctrine, and very full of comfort.

(Confession) Article IX—Justification and Regeneration

We believe we are never accounted righteous before God through our works or merit, but that penitent sinners are justified or accounted righteous before God only by faith in our Lord Jesus Christ.

We believe regeneration is the renewal of man in righteousness through Jesus Christ, by the power of the Holy Spirit, whereby we are made partakers of the divine nature and experience newness of life. By this new birth the believer becomes reconciled to God and is enabled to serve him with the will and the affections.

We believe, although we have experienced regeneration, it is possible to depart from grace and fall into sin; and

we may even then, by the grace of God, be renewed in righteousness.

SCRIPTURAL BASIS: "For by grace are ye saved through faith; and that not of yourselves: it is the gift of God: not of works, lest any man should boast." (Eph. 2:8-9.) "Therefore we conclude that a man is justified by faith without the deeds of the law." (Rom. 3:28.) "Being justified by faith, we have peace with God through our Lord Jesus Christ." (Rom. 5.1.)

This is the great affirmation of Protestantism: JUSTIFICATION BY FAITH. It means that we are justified—that is, made right—by God's grace and not by what we do. Paul emphasized this truth again and again in his letters.

The free, spontaneous love of God is what underlies and starts everything in getting men right with God. "God so loved the world, that he gave his only begotten Son, that whosoever *believeth* in him should not perish, but have everlasting life." For a Christian all righteousness is found *through* and *in* Jesus Christ. He has taken away the "handwriting . . . that was against us, . . . nailing it to his cross" (Col. 2:14).

Personal faith, which means personal trust, is the lever here. "Being justified by *faith*, we have peace with God." Faith is the hand extended to receive God's gift. First God offers, then we believe, then we accept. "By grace are ye saved through faith; and that not of yourselves: it is the gift of God" (Eph. 2:8). If our salvation depended on what we did, how far from it we would be! But as it depends on *what God does*, and what we believe he *can* do, that we are justified by faith becomes, in the quaint language of this article, a "most wholesome doctrine, and very full of comfort."

10. Of Good Works

Although good works, which are the fruits of faith, and follow after justification, cannot put away our sins, and endure the severity of God's judgment; yet are they pleasing and acceptable to God in Christ, and spring out of a true and lively faith, insomuch that by them a lively faith may be as evidently known as a tree is discerned by its fruit.

41

(Confession) Article X—Good Works

We believe good works are the necessary fruits of faith and follow regeneration, but they do not have the virtue to remove our sins or to avert divine judgment. We believe good works, pleasing and acceptable to God in Christ, spring from a true and living faith, for through and by them faith is made evident.

SCRIPTUAL BASIS: "By the deeds of the law there shall no flesh be justified in his sight." (Rom. 3:20.) "Not by works of righteousness which we have done, but according to his mercy he saved us." (Tit. 3:5.) "By grace ye are saved through faith; and that not of yourselves. It is the gift of God." (Eph. 2:8.) "But the fruit of the spirit is love, joy, peace, longsuffering, gentleness, goodness, faith, meekness." (Gal. 5:22.)

The Bible teaches that faith in Christ is the *ground* of salvation, but that good works are the natural expression of that faith. No one can be saved by what he *does*, but those who are saved will wish to do all the good they can.

The above article guards against legalism and trusting in external acts. Nevertheless, it admits that these outward acts, when they spring from sincere hearts, are well pleasing to God. "Grace in the heart is the fountain, the good works are the streams flowing from it.[6]

Methodists were attacked in earlier days by other Protestants who said that the rules and strict discipline of Methodism were really a sort of salvation-by-works process. This charge was unfounded. No people have ever called for clean hearts and converted lives more than the United Methodists; but no people have been more insistent that once having been cleansed in heart and converted in soul by the grace of Christ, the whole of life ought to be so managed and regulated as to bring forth the best and most helpful fruits of faith. We have always taken to heart the command to show our faith by our works.

11. Of Works of Supererogation

Voluntary works—besides, over and above God's commandments—which are called works of supererogation,

[6] *Ibid.*

42

cannot be taught without arrogancy and impiety. For by them men do declare that they do not only render unto God as much as they are bound to do, but that they do more for his sake than of bounden duty is required; whereas Christ saith plainly: When ye have done all that is commanded of you, say, We are unprofitable servants.

SCRIPTURAL BASIS: "Is it any pleasure to the Almighty, that thou art righteous? or is it gain to him, that thou makest thy ways perfect?" (Job 22:3.) "So likewise ye, when ye shall have done all those things which are commanded you, say, We are unprofitable servants: we have done that which was our duty to do." (Luke 17:10.)

The Roman Catholic Church has a teaching against which Article 11 is directed. It holds that there is an immense "treasury of merit," composed of the pious deeds of Christ and of the saints, and that this treasury can be made applicable to the benefit of others. In other words a modern Christian can draw upon the bank account of goodness stored up by others.

The Bible knows nothing of this. The "circle of *duty* takes in the entire ability of man, and therefore leaves no room for the works of supererogation." [7] We can never do enough good anyhow, and each man must stand on his own record and not on that of another.

Incidentally it may be said that out of this Romish doctrine of supererogation came the evil system of selling indulgences —a procedure which so shocked Martin Luther that he began the Reformation in protest against this and other abuses of the Roman Church.

12. Of Sin After Justification

Not every sin willingly committed after justification is the sin against the Holy Spirit, and unpardonable. Wherefore, the grant of repentance is not to be denied to such as fall into sin after justification: after we have received the Holy Spirit, we may depart from grace given,

[7] *Ibid.*

and fall into sin, and, by the grace of God, rise again and amend our lives. And therefore they are to be condemned who say they can no more sin as long as they live here; or deny the place of forgiveness to such as truly repent.

SCRIPTURAL BASIS: "Return, ye backsliding children, and I will heal your backslidings." (Jer. 3:22.) "If any man sin, we have an advocate with the Father, Jesus Christ the righteous." (I John 2:1.) "If we confess our sins, he is faithful and just to forgive us our sins." (I John 1:9.) "Remember therefore from whence thou art fallen, and repent, and do the first works." (Rev. 2:5.)

Certain ancient church fathers held that when a person was forgiven and made a child of God, he was saved forever; but that if he should sin grievously again, he would by that act forfeit every chance to be saved. Article 12 says this is not so. It brushes aside the unreal belief that when a person is once saved, he cannot sin again. Unfortunately he can—as the lives of many have abundantly shown. Our Church, building solidly on experience, holds that just as we may "depart from grace given, and fall into sin," so we may by the same grace "rise again and amend our lives."

This is the well-known falling-from-grace doctrine of Methodism. It admits that even though once completely forgiven, a person can sin again; but asserts that such sin is not unpardonable. Just as one can fall, so one can rise. Isaac Watts wrote:

> And while the lamp holds out to burn,
> The vilest sinner may return.

Nowhere in the Bible can one find any warrant for denying the place of forgiveness to such as truly repent.

Article 12 also opens up the old question of the unpardonable sin. What is it? Many persons have worried greatly for fear they have sinned against the Holy Ghost. Our Methodist fathers, following sound doctrine, have always held that the unpardonable sin is not so much a certain act of willful transgression as it is a long, deliberate, defiance of the Spirit of grace. "The unpardonable state is *in the man,* not in the un-willingness of God to forgive." [8]

Those who worry as to whether they have sinned unpar-donably need worry no more. For those who have really sinned unforgivably will never worry about it. They are already dead spiritually, and after a time even the very grace of God itself, does not reach them. Therefore one who is deeply concerned as to whether or not he has committed the unpardonable sin may be sure that he has *not* committed it.

13. Of the Church

The visible Church of Christ is a congregation of faith-ful men in which the pure Word of God is preached, and the Sacraments duly administered according to Christ's ordinance, in all those things that of necessity are requi-site to the same.

(Confession) Article V—The Church

We believe the Christian Church is the community of all true believers under the Lordship of Christ. We believe it is one, holy, apostolic and catholic. It is the redemptive fellowship in which the Word of God is preached by men divinely called, and the sacraments are duly administered according to Christ's own appoint-ment. Under the discipline of the Holy Spirit the Church exists for the maintenance of worship, the edi-fication of believers and the redemption of the world.

SCRIPTURAL BASIS: "Unto the church of God . . . , to them that are sanctified in Christ Jesus, called to the saints, with all that in every place call upon the name of Jesus Christ our Lord both theirs and ours." (I Cor. 1:2.) "And he gave some, apostles; and some, prophets; and some, evangelists; and some, pastors and teachers; for the perfecting of the saints, for the work of the ministry, for the edifying of the body of Christ." (Eph. 4:11-12.) "The church of God, which he hath purchased with his own blood." (Acts 20:28.)

[8] *Ibid.*

This authoritative definition of the visible Church came to Methodism through the Lutheran and Reformed Church confessions. It makes no attempt to define the Church invisible, that holy and true fellowship whose membership is known to God alone. It speaks of the visible or earthly Church, which it calls first a "congregation." It is not a particular type of priesthood, nor of specially ordained men, but a fellowship of people imbued with Christian faith. This is the apostolic idea. This is the Church of the New Testament.

The true visible Church also hears the "pure Word of God" preached. That is to say, in every real church the gospel in its strength and power is always proclaimed. Likewise in every true church the Sacraments, which were ordained of Christ, are administered according to his direction.

On this definition we stand. Where there are congregations of faithful people, where the pure Word is preached and the Sacraments duly administered, there is the visible Church. United Methodism delights to find true churches among people of all denominations. The faith of the people, the purity of the preached Word, and the due administration of the Sacraments—these things make and mark the Church on earth.

14. Of Purgatory

The Romish doctrine concerning purgatory, pardon, worshiping, and adoration, as well of images as of relics, and also invocation of saints, is a fond thing, vainly invented, and grounded upon no warrant of Scripture, but repugnant to the Word of God.

SCRIPTURAL BASIS: "Who can forgive sins but God only?" (Mark 2:7.) "Thou shalt not make unto thee any graven image." (Exod. 20:4.) "Thou shalt worship the Lord thy God, and him only shalt thou serve." (Matt. 4:10.)

This article is Protestantism's answer to erroneous teachings of the Roman Catholic Church. Purgatory, worshiping images and relics, the priest pronouncing pardon—such beliefs and practices are not found at all in the New Testament and indeed did not come into the Roman Catholic Church until the Middle Ages. There is not a scintilla of evidence in the Scriptures to support the idea of purgatory. The worship and adoration of images and relics, and the invoking of the saints through prayer, are hostile to the whole spirit of Protestantism. Protestantism does respect and venerate holy lives of the past and the present, but it yields worship only to God. "Thou shalt worship the Lord thy God, and him only."

As to pardon we do believe in that, but it is God's pardon, not man's. No priestly absolution can convey what God only can give, for "who can forgive sins but God only?" (Mark 2:7). Our Lord taught us to ask our heavenly Father for forgiveness when we need it—as, sadly enough, we often do. "Our Father, ... forgive us our trespasses."

15. Of Speaking in the Congregation in Such a Tongue as the People Understand

It is a thing plainly repugnant to the Word of God, and the custom of the primitive Church, to have public prayer in the Church, or to administer the Sacraments, in a tongue not understood by the people.

SCRIPTURAL BASIS: "He that speaketh in an unknown tongue speaketh not unto men, but unto God: for no man understandeth him. . . . In the church I had rather speak five words with my understanding . . . than ten thousand words in an unknown tongue." (I Cor. 14:2, 19.)

This was another anti-Catholic article written against the practice of the Roman Church in carrying on its services entirely in Latin. This it did universally until quite recently when there has been more change over into the language of the people. The Reformers, who wrote this particular article, cited the scripture given above against such a practice. They also called attention to the custom of the primitive church in which people certainly did not preach or speak or pray in a language foreign to their life. Origen, an early church father, said in A.D. 202: "The Grecians pray to God in the Greek; the Romans in the Roman; everyone in his own tongue." Religion means nothing at all if it cannot be translated into the life and language and the hearts of people.

16. Of the Sacraments

Sacraments ordained of Christ are not only badges or tokens of Christian men's profession, but rather they are certain signs of grace, and God's good will toward us, by which he doth work invisibly in us, and doth not only quicken, but also strengthen and confirm, our faith in him.

There are two Sacraments ordained of Christ our Lord in the Gospel; that is to say, Baptism and the Supper of the Lord.

Those five commonly called sacraments, that is to say, confirmation, penance, orders, matrimony, and extreme unction, are not to be counted for Sacraments of the Gospel; being such as have partly grown out of the *corrupt* following of the apostles, and partly are states of life allowed in the Scriptures, but yet have not the like nature of Baptism and the Lord's Supper, because they have not any visible sign or ceremony ordained of God.

The Sacraments were not ordained of Christ to be gazed upon, or to be carried about; but that we should duly use them. And in such only as worthily receive the same they have a wholesome effect or operation; but they that receive them unworthily, purchase to themselves condemnation, as St. Paul saith, I Cor. 11:29.

(Confession) Article VI—The Sacraments

We believe the sacraments, ordained by Christ, are symbols and pledges of the Christian's profession and of God's love toward us. They are means of grace by which God works invisibly in us, quickening, strengthening, and confirming our faith in him. Two sacraments are ordained by Christ our Lord, namely, Baptism and the Lord's Supper.

We believe Baptism signifies entrance into the household of faith, and is a symbol of repentance and inner cleansing from sin, a representation of the new birth in Christ Jesus and a mark of Christian discipleship.

We believe children are under the atonement of Christ and as heirs of the Kingdom of God are acceptable subjects for Christian baptism. Children of believing parents through baptism become the special responsibility of the Church. They should be nurtured and led to personal acceptance of Christ, and by profession of faith confirm their baptism.

We believe the Lord's Supper is a representation of our redemption, a memorial of the sufferings and death of Christ, and a token of love and union which Christians have with Christ and with one another. Those who rightly, worthily, and in faith eat the broken bread and drink the blessed cup partake of the body and blood of Christ in a spiritual manner until he comes.

SCRIPTURAL BASIS: Christ ordained but two true sacraments—baptism and the Lord's Supper. (See Matt. 26:26; 28:19; I Cor. 11: 23.) "Go ye therefore, and teach all nations, baptizing them in the name of the Father, and of the Son, and of the Holy Ghost." (Matt. 28:19.) "And as they were eating, Jesus took bread, and blessed it, and brake it, and gave it to the disciples, and said, Take, eat; this is my body." (Matt. 26:26.) "For I have received of the Lord that which also I delivered unto you, That the Lord Jesus the same night in which he was betrayed took bread: and when he had given thanks, he brake it, and said, Take, eat: this is my body, which is broken for you: this do in remembrance of me." (I Cor. 11:23, 24.)

As the next two articles will deal with each of the sacraments, a more complete explanation will be given there. The present article declares what are true sacraments and how these should be reverenced and received.

This particular article mentions other rites and ceremonies which are taken as sacraments by the Roman Catholic Church. Protestants agree that some of these sacred observances are worthy of reverence and respect—for instance, confirmation as well as the rite of ordination into the ministry of the Church, and the ceremony of marriage. These are sacred observances worthy to be hallowed by the good will and prayers of Christian people. Yet, as our articles above state, these rites are not to be counted as equal to the two sacraments ordained by Christ.

Two other rites called sacraments by the Church of Rome, penance and extreme unction, are viewed with distaste by Protestants. Penance, of course, we believe in as a Godly penitence for sin; but it needs no priestly rite to make it effective, and no human being can pronounce forgiveness. Extreme unction, the anointing given by the priest to the dying, may be carried out earnestly and sincerely. However, neither penance nor extreme unction has any warrant in scripture, and they are not sacraments as we understand the term.

17. Of Baptism

Baptism is not only a sign of profession and mark of difference whereby Christians are distinguished from others that are not baptized; but it is also a sign of regeneration or the new birth. The baptism of young children is to be retained in the church. (See Confession's Article VI above for statement on Baptism)

SCRIPTURAL BASIS: "Arise, and be baptized, and wash away thy sins, calling on the name of the Lord." (Acts 22:16.) "Except a man be born of water and of the Spirit, he cannot enter into the kingdom of God." (John 3:5.) "He that believeth and is baptized shall be saved." (Mark 16:16.)

This article calls baptism a *sign* of profession and a *sign* of regeneration—not regeneration itself. To be sure, baptism is an institution of our Lord and so is to be kept and carried out as he commanded. But Protestantism has never put heavy emphasis upon the rite of baptism as having of itself any regenerative value. It signifies something beyond itself. In Christian minds it symbolizes the receiving of the Holy Spirit, and all baptismal prayers uttered by the Church are to the effect that the one who is baptized shall also be baptized with the Holy Spirit.

Our Church holds that the sacrament of baptism ought to

be administered to young children in the name of Christ. It is a token of their initiation into the gospel way and ought to be observed by Christian parents everywhere according to Christ's ordinance. (For further discussion of infant baptism see pages 136-39.)

18. Of the Lord's Supper

The Supper of the Lord is not only a sign of the love that Christians ought to have among themselves one to another, but rather is a sacrament of our redemption by Christ's death; insomuch that, to such as rightly, worthily, and with faith receive the same, the bread which we break is a partaking of the body of Christ; and likewise the cup of blessing is a partaking of the blood of Christ.

Transubstantiation, or the change of the substance of bread and wine in the Supper of our Lord, cannot be proved by Holy Writ, but is repugnant to the plain words of Scripture, overthroweth the nature of a sacrament, and hath given occasion to many superstitions.

The body of Christ is given, taken, and eaten in the Supper, only after a heavenly and spiritual manner. And the means whereby the body of Christ is received and eaten in the Supper is faith.

The Sacrament of the Lord's Supper was not by Christ's ordinance reserved, carried about, lifted up, or worshiped. (*See Confession's Article VI above for statement on the Lord's Supper.*)

Scriptural Basis: "And he took bread, and gave thanks, and brake it, and gave unto them, saying, This is my body which is given for you: this do in remembrance of me. Likewise also the cup after supper, saying, This cup is the new testament in my blood, which is shed for you." (Luke 22:19-20.)

The greatest symbol of the Christian Church is the sacrament of the Lord's Supper. In this Christian people remember what the Lord did for them and pray that in turn they may give themselves as living sacrifices to his service.

In this sacrament the bread and wine—or the elements, as

we commonly call them—signify the body and blood of our Lord Jesus Christ. They are received and eaten in a spiritual, that is, a heavenly, manner; and all the fathers and teachers of the Church have emphasized that the means whereby this is done is *faith*.

There is nothing automatic or mechanical about the Supper of the Lord. He who does not take it reverently and sincerely, or he whose heart is not open by faith, cannot receive its benefits. But when the Lord's Supper is genuinely and seriously entered into with a desire to walk more closely in his holy ways, then indeed it becomes a means of grace and "very full of comfort."

The Roman Catholic doctrine of transubstantiation (which holds that at the word of the priest the bread and wine are miraculously transformed into the actual body and blood of the Lord) is completely repudiated by this article. So also is rejected the idea that the sacrament itself, that is, the elements of the sacrament, have magic properties. It is what happens *within* the believer, not what happens without, that makes for the true sacrament.

19. Of Both Kinds

The cup of the Lord is not to be denied to the lay people; for both the parts of the Lord's Supper, by Christ's ordinance and commandment, ought to be administered to all Christians alike.

SCRIPTURAL BASIS: "He took the cup, and gave thanks, and gave it to them [the disciples], saying, Drink ye all of it." (Matt. 26: 27.) "For as often as ye [believers in common] eat this bread, and drink this cup, ye do shew the Lord's death till he come. . . . But let a man [the believer] examine himself, and so let him eat of that bread, and drink of that cup." (I Cor. 11:26, 28.)

Both the bread and wine were administered by our Lord to his apostles—as all accounts of the original Lord's Supper agree. They were to be given and partaken in remembrance of Christ until his coming again. So the command which we repeat at the Communion service is "Drink ye all of this"—

that is, "All of you, drink." There was never any idea of keeping the cup from the lay people until a comparatively late date in the Roman Catholic Church. Then the Church of Rome, in support of its teaching of transubstantiation, affirmed that the cup need not be given since the "flesh contains the blood." The Roman Catholic Church thereafter ceased to pass the cup to its lay people.

Protestantism gloriously brushes aside all such unwarranted ideas. It insists that lay people and ministers are alike before God and so has restored the idea of a real fellowship or communion. In this neither priest nor minister stands in any way above the people. All together take the bread and wine in remembrance of their risen Lord.

20. Of the One Oblation of Christ, Finished upon the Cross

The offering of Christ, once made, is that perfect redemption, propitiation, and satisfaction for all the sins of the whole world, both original and actual; and there is none other satisfaction for sin but that alone. Wherefore the sacrifice of masses, in the which it is commonly said that the priest doth offer Christ for the quick and the dead, to have remission of pain or guilt, is a blasphemous fable and dangerous deceit.

(Confession) Article VIII—Reconciliation Through Christ

We believe God was in Christ reconciling the world to himself. The offering Christ freely made on the cross is the perfect and sufficient sacrifice for the sins of the whole world, redeeming man from all sin, so that no other satisfaction is required.

SCRIPTURAL BASIS: "So Christ was once offered to bear the sins of many." (Heb. 9:28.) "Knowing that Christ being raised from the dead dieth no more. . . . For in that he died, he died unto sin once." (Rom. 6:9, 10.) "Neither is there salvation in any other: for there is none other name under heaven given among men, whereby we must be saved." (Acts 4:12.) "There remaineth no more sacrifice for sins." (Heb. 10:26.) "After he had offered one

53

sacrifice for sins for ever, [he] sat down on the right hand of God: . . . For by one offering he hath perfected for ever them that are sanctified." (Heb. 10:12, 14.)

This scriptural, Christian view of the sacrifice of Christ is a powerful expression of Protestant faith. It stands as an everlasting denial of the Roman idea that the sacrifice of Christ can be repeated every time the priest says a mass. Methodism, with all Protestantism, holds that what Christ did on Calvary was done once and for all, that his sacrifice was a "full, perfect, and sufficient sacrifice, oblation, and satisfaction for the sins of the whole world." What is done at the Supper of the Lord is in "memory of his precious death until his coming again." No one can ever repeat Christ's sacrifice.

The Roman Catholic doctrine holds that in the Mass the priest has the miraculous power to cause the bread and wine to become the actual body of Christ again, and then he offers Christ's body (and so "says a Mass") for some particular cause or sin. In other words Calvary is supposed to take place again each time the Mass is celebrated.

Our English reformer ancestors repudiated this idea of the mass so completely and so plainly that they used the bluntest of blunt English to describe it: "a blasphemous fable and a dangerous deceit."

21. Of the Marriage of Ministers

The ministers of Christ are not commanded by God's law either to vow the estate of single life, or to abstain from marriage; therefore it is lawful for them, as for all other Christians, to marry at their own discretion, as they shall judge the same to serve best to godliness.

SCRIPTURAL BASIS: The apostle Peter was a married man. "When Jesus was come into Peter's house, he saw his wife's mother laid, and sick of a fever." (Matt. 8:14.) Philip, the evangelist, had "four daughters, virgins, which did prophesy." (Acts 21:9.) Paul says: "A bishop then must be blameless, the husband of one wife" (I Tim. 3:2.) "Let the deacons be the husband of one wife." (I Tim. 3:12.) "Have we not power to lead about . . . a wife, as well as other apostles?" (I Cor. 9:5.)

54

Here is another anti-Romish article, for the Church of Rome has for centuries forbidden its priests to marry. This procedure has no warrant in Scripture. Indeed, Peter, who is claimed by that church to have been the first pope, was a married man; and so were many of the apostles and bishops until a rather late date. Then Rome, keeping its priests cut off from home ties and bound to its own iron discipline, forbade them to marry. Today there is growing agitation against that rule in the Roman Catholic Church, with many priests leaving in order to marry, and strong efforts are being made to have this regulation relaxed.

Protestantism of course follows the practice of the early church. Ministers may marry or not marry according to their own discretion.

22. Of the Rites and Ceremonies of Churches

It is not necessary that rites and ceremonies should in all places be the same, or exactly alike; for they have been always different, and may be changed according to the diversity of countries, times, and men's manners, so that nothing be ordained against God's Word. Whosoever, through his private judgment, willingly and purposely doth openly break the rites and ceremonies of the church to which he belongeth, which are not repugnant to the Word of God, and are ordained and approved by common authority, ought to be rebuked openly (that others may fear to do the like), as one that offendeth against the common order of the church, and woundeth the consciences of weak brethren.

Every particular church may ordain, change, or abolish rites and ceremonies, so that all things may be done to edification.

(Confession) Article XIII—Public Worship

We believe divine worship is the duty and privilege of man who, in the presence of God, bows in adoration, humility and dedication. We believe divine worship is essential to the life of the Church, and that the assembling of the people of God for such worship is necessary to Christian fellowship and spiritual growth.

We believe the order of public worship need not be the same in all places but may be modified by the Church according to circumstances and the needs of men. It should be in a language and form understood by the people, consistent with the Holy Scriptures to the edification of all, and in accordance with the order and discipline of the Church.

SCRIPTURAL BASIS: "As free, and not using your liberty for a cloak of maliciousness, but as the servants of God." (I Pet. 2:16.) "Let every man be fully persuaded in his own mind." (Rom. 14:5.) "Let all things be done unto edifying." (I Cor. 14:26.)

The breadth and freedom of the Christian faith is made clear in Article 22 of The Articles of Religion and in Article XIII of The Confession of Faith. These recognize frankly that in different countries and places Christians will have different ways of worship. Such divergence is to be approved. Every church, therefore, is allowed to have the right to change its rites and ceremonies as it pleases so long as "all things [are] done to edification"—in other words so long as all things are agreeable to true Christian faith and its expression.

Let it be noted that the privilege of ordering and arranging rites and ceremonies belongs to a *church*, not to an *individual*. For the article goes on to say that "whosoever, *through his private judgment*, willingly and purposely doth openly break the rites and ceremonies of the church to which he belongeth" ought to be rebuked. Thus the church itself may establish and change its own rites and ceremonies, but no private individual is allowed to do so. This provision of the article is sometimes overlooked.

23. Of the Rulers of the United States of America

The President, the Congress, the general assemblies, the governors, and the councils of state *as the delegates of the people*, are the rulers of the United States of America, according to the division of power made to them by the Constitution of the United States and by the constitutions of their respective states. And the said states are a sovereign and independent nation, and ought not to be subject to any foreign jurisdiction.

(Confession) Article XVI—Civil Government

We believe civil government derives its just powers from the sovereign God. As Christians we recognize the governments under whose protection we reside and believe such governments should be based on, and be responsible for, the recognition of human rights under God. We believe war and bloodshed are contrary to the gospel and spirit of Christ. We believe it is the duty of Christian citizens to give moral strength and purpose to their respective governments through sober, righteous and godly living.

SCRIPTURAL BASIS: "Render therefore unto Caesar the things which are Caesar's; and unto God the things that are God's." (Matt. 22: 21.) "Let every soul be subject unto the higher powers. For there is no power but of God: the powers that be are ordained of God. . . . For rulers are not a terror to good works, but to the evil. . . . For he is the minister of God to thee for good." (Rom. 13:1, 3, 4.)

When John Wesley sent over twenty-four Articles of Religion to American Methodism, he selected them one by one from the Thirty-nine Articles of the Church of England. Now among the Thirty-nine Articles is one which certifies to the faith of the Church of England in the supremacy of the king. Wesley, who knew that America had won its liberty from the British king, therefore omitted this article entirely. But the Methodist fathers in organizing the Methodist Episcopal Church at the Christmas Conference felt that there ought to be in the faith of the new church some reference to the rulers of the land. So they wrote the present Article 23, declaring that the President, the Congress, and the various authorities named are the "rulers of the United States." They also backed up the Declaration of Independence—only a few years old at that time—by declaring the United States to be sovereign and independent. Church and state are separate in America, but The United Methodist Church *makes the in-*

57

dependence and sovereignty of the United States part of its fundamental faith.

In Methodist churches established in other lands outside the United States, it has been found advisable to change or adapt this article so as to affirm recognition of the established authorities in each such land.

24. Of Christian Men's Goods

The riches and goods of Christians are not common, as touching the right, title, and possession of the same, as some do falsely boast. Notwithstanding, every man ought, of such things as he possesseth, liberally to give alms to the poor, according to his ability.

(Confession) Article XV—The Christian and Property

We believe God is the owner of all things and that the individual holding of property is lawful and is a sacred trust under God. Private property is to be used for the manifestation of Christian love and liberality, and to support the Church's mission in the world. All forms of property, whether private, corporate or public, are to be held in solemn trust and used responsibly for human good under the sovereignty of God.

SCRIPTURAL BASIS: The commandment "Thou shalt not steal" (Exod. 20:15) implies ownership of property. "Give to him that asketh thee, and from him that would borrow of thee turn not thou away." (Matt. 5:42.) Giving and lending also necessarily imply the personal ownership of property. "But whoso hath this world's good, and seeth his brother have need, and shutteth up his bowels of compassion from him, how dwelleth the love of God in him?" (I John 3:17.)

Article 24 of the Articles of Religion and Article XV of the Confession of Faith, as they deal with economics, are of great import. They were written in opposition to the teaching advanced by certain groups in Europe just after the Reformation to the effect that Christian people have no inherent right to be the owners of private property. To be a Christian, they said, one must divide all that one has with all other people. This

58

of course is communism, though the system that went by that name in earlier times was different in its ideals from modern dictator-dominated communism.

It is quite true that the early Christians did for a time have "all things [in] common," as the book of Acts tells us (4:32). But this plan did not work with as saintly a group as the early Christians, and it will not work any better today. A communistic society can never operate unless its will is enforced by a ruthless police power, which is the very breath of life to such a system.

Our Christian forebears in Europe considered this article necessary as an affirmation that each Christian *does* have a right to his own possessions. Our church teaches that the title to one's private property is inherent in the individual. However, these Articles above guard against a rapacious capitalism by affirming that every man out of his (private) possessions must give to the poor according to his ability—meaning that each Christian must share with others. Neither communism nor a selfish possessiveness is therefore the Christian answer, but *stewardship,* in which each man truly and rightfully owns his own goods and values, but holds them *in trust for God and his fellow man.* In other words our goods are ours to make them God's.

25. Of a Christian Man's Oath

As we confess that vain and rash swearing is forbidden Christian men by our Lord Jesus Christ and James his apostle; so we judge that the Christian religion doth not prohibit, but that a man may swear when the magistrate requireth, in a cause of faith and charity, so it be done according to the prophet's teaching, in justice, judgment, and truth.

SCRIPTURAL BASIS: "And thou shalt swear, The Lord liveth, in truth, in judgment, and in righteousness." (Jer. 4:2.) "Men verily swear by the greater: and an oath for confirmation is to them an end of all strife." (Heb. 6:16.) "And Jonathan caused David to swear again." (I Sam. 20:17.) "I call God for a record upon my soul." (II Cor. 1:23.)

59

The Quakers and other sects, at the time this article was written, did not believe that it was right to swear an oath before a magistrate. They took our Lord's injunction "Swear not at all" to be a direct command against affirming anything at law. Our church holds that rash and vain swearing is forbidden, of course, by the New Testament; but we "judge," as the fathers here put it, that the Christian religion does not keep a man from taking a solemn oath when a magistrate requireth it "in a cause of faith and charity."

A Christian's oath, however, ought to be given reverently in justice, in judgment, and in truth. Lightness or levity in making affirmations, or in stating what one cannot know to be true—all this is forbidden by the Word of God and the common sense of the Christian brotherhood.

There are two articles in the Confession of Faith as this was formulated by the Evangelical United Brethren Church, which are not exactly in parallel with any of the traditional Methodist articles. One of these, Article XIV deals with the Lord's Day. We give its text below. The other is Article XI on Sanctification and Christian Perfection. This last we will cite and discuss in our next chapter on special beliefs under the heading, "The Possibility of Final Perfection." See it there.

(Confession) Article XIV—The Lord's Day

We believe the Lord's Day is divinely ordained for private and public worship, for rest from unnecessary work, and should be devoted to spiritual improvement, Christian fellowship, and service. It is commemorative of our Lord's resurrection and is an emblem of our eternal rest. It is essential to the permanence and growth of the Christian Church, and important to the welfare of the civil community.[1]

[1] Note: For a discussion of the Lord's Day and its meaning for a present-day Christian, see page 77.

CHAPTER THREE

Prominent Doctrines

METHODISM has emphasized certain Christian doctrines so heavily that they have come to be regarded by some as distinctively Methodist. These are:

REGENERATION—The new birth, through which one becomes a child of God.

THE WITNESS OF THE SPIRIT—The certification which each Christian may have that he is a child of God.

THE POSSIBILITY OF FINAL PERFECTION—The teaching that it is possible and intended that everyone shall live a sinless life and be "made perfect in love" in this life.

Other doctrines also greatly stressed have been:

REPENTANCE—A godly sorrow for sin coupled with a will to sin no more. Repentance of course must precede any complete turning to God.

UNIVERSAL REDEMPTION—That Christ died for all, not simply a chosen number.

JUSTIFICATION BY FAITH—The great affirmation of the Protestant Reformation. This has been, and is, a Methodist doctrine as it is for all who rightly walk in the Christian way. Its meaning has been explained under Article 9, page 40.

Regeneration

The New Birth, as Christians have long called it, is that act of God through which one is brought into his kingdom and experiences a change of heart. In the Scripture this experience is described as being "born again."

SCRIPTURAL BASIS: "Jesus . . . said. . . , Verily, I say unto thee, Except a man be born again, he cannot see the kingdom of God." (John 3:3.) "Being born again, not of corruptible seed, but of incorruptible, by the word of God, which liveth and abideth forever." (I Pet. 1:23.) "If any man be in Christ, he is a new creature." (II Cor. 5:17.) . . . "Which were born, not of blood, nor of the will of the flesh, nor of the will of man, but of God." (John 1:13.) "That ye put on the new man, which after God is created in righteousness and true holiness." (Eph. 4:24.)

There is a very real sense in which this doctrine, or rather the truth it affirms, is the foundation of everything for a Christian. For unless and until a person becomes a Christian, how can he live a Christian life? How can he be heir to all Christian beliefs and promises? It has been the cardinal fallacy of the Church and ministry through the ages to treat as Christians those who in reality are not Christians, and to expect from such persons all Christian graces and attainments when they had never become Christian in the first place. "Ye must be born again" is the injunction that underlies every other Christian command.

But this becoming a Christian is not something one does for himself but something that God does for him. Each person, to be sure, must cooperate by repenting of his past sins and sincerely intend to lead a new life and sin no more. He must believe that God can and will save him—so much each one must do if he would find God, or rather, have God find him.

But the giving of a new spiritual life, the actual regenerative act, is by the power of God and God alone. Souls are born anew not "of the will of the flesh, nor of the will of man, but of God," as John says (1:13). The Church itself lacks regenerative power. It can receive a person into its fellowship by an outward act of reception; it can baptize one and pray that "he may be numbered with God's people here, and with his saints in glory everlasting"; it can put his name on its roll and make him feel at home—but the actual creative work, the dynamic work, the regenerative work of quickening one who has been "dead in trespasses and sin"—that belongs to God.

"How can this be?" Nicodemus asked Jesus when Jesus told him that a person had need to be born again.

"The wind blows where it wills," replied the Master, "and you hear the sound of it, but you do not know whence it comes or whither it goes; so it is with every one who is born of the Spirit." (John 3:8 R.S.V.)

Life and scripture both join here to give undeniable testimony. The New Testament is filled with the accounts of those who were taken by God to become his children. So is the history of the Church, past and present. All revivals of religion have emphasized the new birth. No ceremony nor churchly process nor official pronouncement can ever be substituted for it.

A caution, however, can here be given. Being regenerate and born again is one thing; *knowing exactly when* one has been born again is something else. Many sincere Christians have not been able to tell when they became Christians. But they know they *are*.

It is at this point that certain earnest evangelists of early days, and some today, are inclined to be dogmatic. "If you don't know when you were saved, you are not saved," was the way these people put it. This is not sound reasoning. A clear thinker once countered this statement by saying, "If you don't remember when you were born, you never have been born at all"—which is ridiculous of course, as he meant it to be.

The truth is, human temperament seems to have something to do with the type of conversion experienced—that is, with one's regeneration. Persons who are of strong, decisive makeup usually have a cataclysmic conversion—that is, a soul-shaking one—if they are converted at all. Like the apostle Paul, who was of that type, they get knocked down, as it were, by the roadside and have their lives suddenly reversed. Of course such persons never forget the day nor hour. Augustine and John Wesley were other leaders of the Church who could point to a definite soul-shaking experience. So can many preachers and sincere laymen.

63

But there are quieter, more even-tempered persons, like Tertullian, the Christian thinker, who said that he "had a mind naturally religious" from his youth up. Such people usually grow in grace from childhood, and God's regenerative work, like the growing of the grass or the opening of the flowers in the spring, is almost imperceptible in degree, though glorious in its full fruition.

The important thing is for each person, of whatever type, to *know* that he has "passed from death unto life" and is a child of God. Whether by crisis or "lysis," as a doctor of medicine once put it; by a sudden explosive change or by a gradual one, just so that we have become God's children—that is the essential thing.

The Witness of the Spirit

SCRIPTURAL BASIS: "The Spirit itself beareth witness with our spirit, that we are the children of God." (Rom. 8:16.) "He that believeth on the Son of God hath the witness in himself." (I John 5:10.) "Because ye are sons, God hath sent forth the Spirit of his Son into your hearts, crying, Abba, Father." (Gal. 4:6.) "The love of God is shed abroad in our hearts by the Holy Ghost." (Rom. 5:5.) "The fruit of the Spirit is love, joy, peace, longsuffering, gentleness, goodness, faith, meekness, temperance." (Gal. 5:22-23.)

Here is another Christian truth of great import—the Witness of the Spirit. It means that the Holy Spirit in the heart of a believer can and does give him a firsthand assurance that he is a child of God. Paul stated this truth in his never-to-be forgotten words, "The Spirit itself beareth witness with our spirit, that we are the children of God." The apostle knew, as he wrote this passage, that all other Christians would understand exactly what he meant.

United Methodists, with other Christians, rejoice, as did the apostle, in the knowledge that God does certify unmistakably to each believer when his salvation is sure. But because this idea has sometimes been considered presumptuous or misguided, or may rise from inward feelings which have no basis in outward fact, it has been heavily attacked by many Christian thinkers. John Wesley himself, while he preached and taught the truth of the divine witness, was very careful to say exactly what he meant by it.

"By the testimony of the Spirit," he wrote, "I mean, an inward impression on the soul, whereby the Spirit of God immediately and directly witnesses to my spirit, that I am a child of God; that Jesus Christ hath loved me, and given Himself for me; that all my sins are blotted out, and I, even I, am reconciled to God."

The real question here is: Can a man truly *know* that he is a child of God? Not can a man *hope* so or *think* so. Can he *know?* Methodism with all the force of personal testimony has put together Bible doctrine and its own experience to say that one certainly can. Let us look at this a bit more.

The witness of the Spirit does not discount the fact that there are many things a Christian can learn for himself by study of the Bible and by living the Christian life. For instance, a person knows when he is doing right, when he is following the laws of God, when he has a good conscience, when with mind and strength and heart and soul he is endeavoring to follow God's holy will and commandment. Common sense tells one whether he is or is not in line with the purposes of God.

But what the witness of the Spirit means is that above and beyond the testimony of one's own conscience something else comes in—something tremendous—even the "testimony of God's Spirit, which is superadded to and conjoined" to one's own, Wesley put it.

It is at this point that a crass world begins to demur. "It is all right to *hope* and *reason* that you are a child of God," it is said, "but to be *sure* of it and to say that God makes you sure, that is to claim more than one has a right to claim."

It certainly is claiming a great deal, but those who have felt the inner witness have never doubted. They admit that there may be enthusiasts who imagine they have received blessings which perhaps they have not received, that there may be erratic persons who make all sorts of claims which are not "according to knowledge." Wesley himself wrote, "How many

65

have mistaken the voice of their own imagination for this 'witness of the Spirit of God,' and thence idly presumed they were the children of God, while they were doing the works of the devil? These are truly and properly enthusiasts." But the same Wesley went on to say the "testimony of the Spirit [is] an inward impression on the soul, whereby the Spirit of God immediately and directly witnesses to my spirit, that I am a child of God"—the quotation of Wesley which has just been cited on the previous page.

Wesley admits, however (after all his explanation), that "he who hath that witness in himself, cannot explain it to one who hath it not." He even adds "Nor indeed is it to be expected that he should." But it can be preached, it can be taught, it can be claimed by those who have felt it, and it can be received, and we dare say it is, by those who sincerely and earnestly pray God for it. "If ye then, being evil, know how to give good gifts unto your children: how much more shall your heavenly Father give the Holy Spirit to them that ask him?" (Luke 11:13.)

Perhaps not all Christians have received the witness of the Spirit; perhaps God has not chosen to give it to each and every one—for the divine witness is not something we can wrest from heaven by force, nor take from God by pressing certain spiritual buttons. It is a priceless divine gift, albeit one that has been promised to those who diligently seek for it.

A man once joined a fraternal order in which after an initiation the new member was always presented with a badge of his fellowship. But when the secretary of the lodge went to get the badge, he was embarrassed to find that the supply had become exhausted. "I am sorry," he said to the newly initiated brother; "we let our supply run out. But we will write right away and get some more. Don't forget to claim yours in a few days, for you have got it coming to you."

A weak illustration perhaps, but the sincere Christian can feel with due reverence that he has "coming to him" the Gift of the Spirit. Let him seek until he finds, knock and keep on knocking until the gift is given, and then he with the Christians of the ages will *know*. Seek it, brother and sister, seek it. And when you find it, you will need no book to tell you what we are talking about.

Universal Redemption

SCRIPTURAL BASIS: "That he by the grace of God should taste death for every man." (Heb. 2:9.) "He is the propitiation for our sins: and not for ours only, but also for the sins of the whole world." (I John 2:2.) "The grace of God that bringeth salvation hath appeared to all men." (Tit. 2:11.) "God so loved the world, that he gave his only begotten Son, that whosoever believeth in him should not perish, but have everlasting life." (John 3:16.) "God our Saviour . . . will have all men to be saved." (I Tim. 2:3-4.)

Universal redemption was the teaching that Methodism proclaimed eagerly and gladly in its formative years when it was up against the Calvinistic doctrine that Christ had died for the elect only, or for those only who were foreordained to be saved. Calvinism, always strong on logic, said that since only the elect were saved, the death of Christ and the redemption he brought was for them and them only—for who else got it?

Brushing this reasoning away as words which darken counsel, United Methodists took up the resounding slogan "Universal Redemption" as a sort of war cry. Christ died for every man, not a select group—this was the affirmation that caught the ear of the multitudes who thronged the commons of England and packed the log chapels of the American frontier to hear the Methodists preach. Charles Wesley sang:

> O for a trumpet voice,
>   On all the world to call!
> To bid their hearts rejoice
>   In him who died for all!
> For all my Lord was crucified;
> For all, for all my Saviour died.

Hope and promise, not for a few but for everyone, rang out in such hymns and in such preaching.

Universal redemption is not preached so often today, simply

67

because it is not doubted now as it once was. The battle against that aspect of ironclad predestination has been completely won. Therefore, while we hold this doctrine as solidly as ever, we do not affirm it constantly as once we did because we do not need to. But if it were to be challenged again, we would renew the battle as energetically as ever.

Falling from Grace

In this brief outline of special United Methodist beliefs a word more should be said about falling from grace. The "possibility of final apostasy" is the technical name for the unlovely fact that even the best of Christians may lose what they have.

It is surprising that falling from grace, which is at best a negative situation, should have been held up as such a positive doctrine of Methodism. That is, it would be surprising if falling from grace were not so palpably true in real life. In my treatment of the Articles of Religion and Confession of Faith I mentioned those unrealistic persons who believe that "once in grace, always in grace"—that when Christ saves a person, that person always afterward stays saved. Would that he might! United Methodists with all Christians would rejoice to believe that no man who has ever come to Christ can ever fall away. But alas for the weakness of human nature and the power of sin! "Watch ye and pray, lest ye enter into temptation," was the Lord's constant injunction to his own. "Lead us not into temptation, but deliver us from evil."

Instance after instance both in scripture and in life have occurred where those who have once tasted of God's salvation have later grown cold and fallen away. Even Paul was afraid "lest that by any means, when I have preached to others, I myself should be a castaway." Man can fall, we must admit; but man can rise again. United Methodism does not blink the facts here but with all Christians hopes all things, at the same time singing her great war song:

> My soul, be on thy guard;
> Ten thousand foes arise;

The hosts of sin are pressing hard,
To draw thee from the skies.

Ne'er think the victory won,
Nor lay thine armor down;
The work of faith will not be done,
Till thou obtain the crown.

Christian Perfection

Over against this negative and unlovely truth United Methodism teaches what is called in technical language the "possibility of final perfection," or Christian perfection, as it is usually called.

This was the cardinal doctrine and daily pursuit of early Methodism—the ceaseless, unremitting endeavor to live a sinless life. Is it possible to live such a life when "all have sinned, and come short of the glory of God?" United Methodists have always maintained not only that it is possible but that it is necessary to "follow . . . holiness, without which no man shall see the Lord" (Heb. 12:14); that God's commands are given to be obeyed, else they would not be given at all; and that God would but mock us had he given us commandments which he knew we could not possibly keep.

John Wesley taught that it was possible for a person to live every day in such a manner as to be blameless before God and man. He held that it was possible for one to be made "perfect in love" while he yet lived, and asked every preacher who joined the Methodist Conference to answer this question: "Do you expect to be made perfect in love in this life?" Philip Otterbein and Jacob Albright also asked each preacher this same question. That question is still asked of every preacher before he joins one of our United Methodist conferences today. What exactly does it mean?

It does not mean that people should expect to be mentally or physically perfect while they live or that they can ever reach a state spiritually where there is no possibility of falling into sin. "Perfection," as W. E. Sangster of London once expressed it, "is an unfortunate term." It has about it an idea of something that is finished and fixed. That is not what the

Christian means by this idea. He means that if we can live one day without sin, we can live two; if two, then many—why not all? So there can be a growing in grace and a drawing closer and closer to God each day until the time arrives when one literally becomes what God would have him be—and is not that a perfect man?

Wesley never claimed for himself that he had been "made perfect in [Christian] love," and some who have claimed it have been most clearly mistaken about themselves. But if God can by one creative act cause souls to be born into his kingdom, may not his grace, having daily sway in his people's lives, eventually fit them for living ever at home with him in the fullness and richness of his kingdom? Whether this comes by a single creative touch while one lives or in the life everlasting is in God's hands.

At any rate the doctrine of Christian perfection has been the one specific doctrinal contribution which Methodism has made to the Church universal. John Wesley called it the "peculiar doctrine committed to our trust." In all else we have been, as we should be, glad and energetic followers in the main stream of Christian belief. But in this one doctrine we stand by ourselves and utter a teaching that reaches up fearlessly and touches the very Scepter of God. Nerved by the tremendous, "Be ye holy; for I am holy," and "Be ye therefore perfect, even as your father which is in heaven is perfect," we are to hope for ourselves and for others that we shall be made perfect in love in this life. And perhaps here again, as is our faith, so shall it be.

United Methodism's official statement on this doctrine is found in Article XI of her Confession of Faith. It is a clear, strong, and beautifully balanced explanation of this doctrine, and the Evangelical United Brethren who brought this into United Methodism are to be thanked by all for formulating it so admirably:

Article XI—Sanctification and Christian Perfection

We believe sanctification is the work of God's grace through the Word and the Spirit, by which those who have been born again are cleansed from sin in their thoughts, words, and acts, and are enabled to live in accordance with God's will, and to strive for holiness without which no one will see the Lord.

Entire sanctification is a state of perfect love, righteousness and true holiness which every regenerate believer *may obtain* by being delivered from the power of sin, by loving God with all the heart, soul, mind and strength, and by loving one's neighbor as one's self. Through faith in Jesus Christ this gracious gift may be received in this life both gradually and instantaneously, and should be sought earnestly by every child of God.

We believe this experience does not deliver us from the infirmities, ignorance, and mistakes common to man, nor from the possibilities of further sin. The Christian must continue on guard against spiritual pride and seek to gain victory over every temptation to sin. He must respond wholly to the will of God so that sin will lose its power over him; and the world, the flesh, and the devil are put under his feet. Thus he rules over these enemies with watchfulness through the power of the Holy Spirit.

Evangelism and the Evangelistic Spirit

Closely connected with the doctrinal beliefs of United Methodism has been its aggressive way of presenting them. This means evangelism and reaching the unreached. So energetically was the gospel pressed upon all by our United Methodist forebears that Methodism came to be regarded as primarily an evangelistic movement—which it largely is. Always the evangelizing principle has been at the heart of it.

Methods of evangelizing vary; but the gospel is carried forward today, as in the past, primarily by the voice of man communicating the truths of God to other persons. The pulpit through its preachers and teachers has led the way; but sincere laymen and women of the Church, as they have spoken to other men and women, have played, and continue to play, a very great part.

There are two methods of evangelizing which the Church has

used with success. First and perhaps most effective, especially during Methodism's formative years, was *revival preaching*. The other method has been indicated above—that of personal approach by person to person. This last is often carried on today as *visitation evangelism*. Both methods hold great promise; both have had large results.

Evangelistic services and preaching missions have been wonderfully used by United Methodism to express and implement its evangelistic zeal. Revivals, as such services were formerly called because of their announced intent, were really concentrated, intensive efforts to spread the gospel by setting apart periods for preaching to church people, and for calling sinners and "outsiders" to change their lives. Such periods have been of inestimable benefit.

Revival and evangelistic services are marked by:

1. Preaching which emphasizes and hammers away upon the absolute fundamentals of Christian life and duty—sin and its consequences, Christ as Savior, Redeemer, and Lord of all life.

2. Direct pleas to lukewarm and indifferent church members to recapture the lost radiancy of faith and an even more direct plea to those afar from God to come to him and find life sweet and purposeful.

Such services have a certain cumulative effect. One sermon follows another; each plea intensifies those that have gone before. The net result is the stirring up of the church to greater activity and zeal and the conversion of sinners through the work of reclaiming grace.

Every local church needs periods when people are summoned to sit under strong gospel preaching; when they are urged to bring outsiders with them and to give, when opportunity allows, a sincere statement of what Christ means to them. Our church believes that it has the right to expect each professing Christian to take his or her place, when called upon to do so, in the firing line for God. Church school teachers especially have a great opportunity here.

Visitation evangelism does not necessarily depend on periods of revival preaching for its effective work, though intensive preaching and the personal work of devoted Christian visitors go together and support each other. The visitation method has the advantage of reaching those who would never think of going within the walls of a church. It also gives an opportunity to laymen to reach the unreached by private personal appeal. Many a lay person, often to his own surprise, has proved to be unusually talented and successful as a visitation evangelist. Indeed visitation evangelism is largely a lay movement in present-day United Methodism. The pastor gives inspiration and direction in all well-organized plans, but the laymen are the evangelizers—as was true in the days of the apostles.

In all evangelizing two things are needed:

First, a sure knowledge on the part of the one who carries the message of the things of which he speaks. He must get over to other persons not something he has read in a book or heard from a pulpit, but something he has experienced in life. Of course he or she has read the gospel story and heard gospel preaching and knows what others have said. But beyond all else there is the tremendous affirmation "I know," which is the strength of anyone who would help another find the way to God.

Second, the true evangelist must have an earnest desire that others will know and experience God's grace also. He is anxious to tell this message and see others converted. This used to be called a "concern for souls." It is always powerful within those who are conscious that God has done something in their own lives.

The United Methodist Church intends today as in the past to continue its evangelistic efforts. To be sure, new techniques may be called for; but there is no substitute for presenting the word of God to man boldly, strongly, and pleadingly.

A church without revivals and conference areas where the revival spirit has died away are like troops doing cantonment duty—sitting down to routine garrison occupation. Where the gospel is preached and where sinners are called to repentance, where personal workers go out, and where men and women really are brought back from death unto life, there the Church becomes glorious in its spiritual militancy. "Are we going to settle down and be simply an army of occupation?" an aggressive Methodist layman once challenged his fellows in the midst of an evangelistic campaign. "Or are we going to lead a cavalry charge?"

Other great denominations have copied United Methodism in its methods of evangelism; and when they have, they have benefited amazingly. It will be tragic if we who have been great revivalists and evangelists shall forget our former ways. With all the crudeness and blatancy which have been displayed by certain evangelists, with all the crass, brassy showmanship which has been used, with all the pillorying of people's inmost feelings as they have been held up to public view, the revivalist and the evangelist can claim genuine converts by the thousands. It is true that many fall away after the heightened emotion of the revival period passes, but it is also true that many remain who have been turned from evil unto righteousness and who live ever after as examples that God's power can make bad people good.

"Evangelize or die" is the message that two thousand years of Christian history writes indelibly over the altar of every church.

CHAPTER FOUR

Discipline

DOCTRINE has to do with what one believes, discipline with what one does. Every Christian must follow certain principles of good conduct just as surely as he must hold to principles of true belief.

As was stated on an earlier page, the very name "Methodist" was given to the little group led by John Wesley because they were so methodical in the way they did things. It was their conviction that a good life ought to be made to count for God by what it does as well as by what it believes. So "discipline" has been a big word in Methodism. In the very beginning a series of rules was laid down by Wesley in order to teach his people how they might profitably use their time.

Wesley's rules are known as the GENERAL RULES. They are published in every issue of our book of *Discipline*; they are fixed in the written constitution of The United Methodist Church (and not one of them can be changed except by amending the constitution—a long, difficult, and unlikely process). While our interpretation of these rules is somewhat different from that of our fathers, they are still the official rules of our Church; and they have always provided a systematic guide for Christian conduct.

Wesley drew up the General Rules in 1739 at the request of certain members of the Methodist societies. They asked him to give them a definite plan for Christian living. This he did, and from that day to this, the General Rules have been at the heart of the Methodist movement.

While we shall follow in this chapter the general outline of

75

Wesley's General Rules, it should be noted that the *Discipline* of the Evangelical Church included "General and Special Rules for Members of the Church" (Part II); and that the *Discipline* of the United Brethren Church included the "Duties of Members" of the Church (Section II) to the time of the union in 1946. The *Discipline* of the Evangelical United Brethren Church included the "Duties of Members" and "Spiritual Culture." These are very similar to Wesley's General Rules.

The General Rules were not intended to be a complete system of Christian ethics. They presuppose that every Christian already knows right and wrong when it comes to great matters of Christian morality. Wesley gave no rule against murder or theft or adultery because he did not need to. United Methodists, with all other Christians, are expected to live in line with God's Word at all times. What the General Rules do is emphasize and pinpoint Christian morality at stressful places in a methodical, practical, biblical way.

It may be worth noting that while our United Methodist doctrine is quite broad, its discipline has been thought by many to be extremely narrow. Especially in early days Methodists were considered "narrow" because of their strict manner of life. Even within the church itself there have been those who have complained from time to time over certain strict interpretations of the General Rules. But life and experience provided the final test, and no present-day United Methodist need be ashamed of the result in character that came by obeying these time-honored rules.

The General Rules fall into three divisions. The first division may be called the *negative* rules. These represent those actions and those attitudes which a Christian must not take. Wesley explained as an introduction to this section that every Christian must first of all avoid evil of every kind, especially "that which is most generally practiced." Then he proceeded to tell the various things which represent the doing of positive evil.

The second division of the General Rules is *positive*. Christians must do all the good they can. Wesley here lists many Christian acts and procedures which are to be followed.

The third division enjoins *attendance upon all the ordinances*

76

of God, such as public worship, Holy Communion, prayer (both at home and in public), Bible reading, and fasting. This is where the churchliness of United Methodism comes in.

Let us now examine the General Rules and their present-day application.

The Negative Rules

RULE ONE

[Against] the taking of the name of God in vain

SCRIPTURAL BASIS: "Thou shalt not take the name of the Lord thy God in vain; for the Lord will not hold him guiltless that taketh his name in vain." (Exod. 20:7.)

This supports the Third Commandment. Cursing, swearing, and railing against God on the part of profane people have always been discountenanced among Christians everywhere. Modern church people sometimes have become careless in the way they use expletives and current explosive terms. Psychologically such expletives furnish something of relief, so the psychiatrists tell us; and within their degree harmless expressions of vehemence do no ill. But the name of God should not be brought into common conversation except in a most reverent way. "Thou shalt not take the name of the Lord thy God in vain" must be written anew today.

RULE TWO

[Against] the profaning the day of the Lord, either by doing ordinary work therein, or by buying or selling

SCRIPTURAL BASIS: The essential moral import of the Fourth Commandment has always been reflected in Christianity. "Remember the sabbath day, to keep it holy." (Exod. 20:8.) (See article in Confession of Faith, page 60.)

Let it be noted that Wesley referred to Sunday as the "day of the Lord," not the "sabbath." Puritanical legalism which would transfer to the Christian Sunday all the heavy burdens of the Jewish dispensation need not burden or weigh us down today. Nevertheless there is a sense in which the Lord's Day has been hallowed eternally by the resurrection of Christ and is to be kept in his name and for his glory and for the life and well-being of his Church. The Christian Church and the Christian Sunday stand together; injure one and you injure the other.

A discerning writer some years ago said that if he were given control of American life, he would first of all restore the old-fashioned Sunday. "For," said he, "the old-fashioned Sunday was the best remedy ever devised to restore peace and sobriety to a jittery world."

In our time Sunday has come to be a day of recreation and within reason is one in which family life and home life can be developed and enjoyed in a quiet, Christian way.

Let it be admitted that of necessity there are some businesses which must be carried out on Sunday as well as on other days. But let us remember Sunday to keep it holy, not because of crystallized legality, but because of the richness and grace made possible by the day of our Lord.

Buying and selling on Sunday are specifically forbidden by this rule and forbidden, too, by the deeper conscience of Christian men and women. Sunday should refit us for the six days in which we must labor. To do that, it must be a day especially dedicated to the worship and the remembrance of Almighty God.

RULE THREE

[Against] drunkenness, buying or selling spirituous liquors, or drinking them, unless in cases of extreme necessity

SCRIPTURAL BASIS: The wisdom literature of the Bible condemns strong drink. "Be not among winebibbers; . . . for the drunkard and the glutton shall come to poverty." (Prov. 23:20-21.) "Wine is a mocker, strong drink is raging. . . . At the last it biteth like a serpent, and stingeth like an adder." (Prov. 20:1; 23:32.) The New Testament puts drinking in the whole context of the Christian life, where it sees it as evil. "Let us walk honestly. . . . not in rioting and drunkenness. . . . But put ye on the Lord Jesus Christ." (Rom.

13:13-14.) "We are not of the night. . . . Therefore . . . let us watch and be sober." (I Thess. 5:5-6.) "Nor thieves, . . . nor drunkards, . . . shall inherit the kingdom of God." (I Cor. 6:10.)

From the very beginning our people have been a temperate people and have been opposed with all their hearts and souls to the buying and selling of intoxicating liquor. To be sure, in, this rule Wesley made a distinction between spirituous liquors and presumably those which had been brewed. But the modern Methodist should reject any distinction of this sort. The milder liquors lead on to the stronger ones, and there is something about the earnest Christian life which reacts violently against any kind of intoxicating drink. All theories go down before the terrific fact that every day lives are being wasted and ruined by strong drink. Let it not be tolerated by us!

RULE FOUR

[Against] slaveholding; buying or selling slaves

This rule was added in the United States in 1789 as by that time slavery had there become a burning moral issue. Today since the judgment of both God and man condemn slavery everywhere, this rule is of no more than historic interest.

RULE FIVE

[Against] fighting, quarreling, brawling, brother going to law with brother; returning evil for evil, or railing for railing; the using of many words in buying or selling

SCRIPTURAL BASIS: "From whence come wars and fightings among you?—come they not hence, even of your lusts that war in your members?" (Jas. 4:1). "Now the works of the flesh are manifest which are these; . . . hatred, variance, emulations, wrath, strife, seditions, heresies." (Gal. 5:19, 20.) "Dare any of you, having a matter against another, go to law before the unjust, and not before the saints? Do ye not know that the saints shall judge the world?" (I Cor. 6:1-2.) "Not rendering evil for evil, or railing for railing: but contrariwise blessing." (I Pet. 3:9.) "Let your conversation be without covetousness." (Heb. 13:5.) "But let your yea be yea; and your nay, nay; lest ye fall into condemnation." (Jas. 5:12.)

79

The whole gospel of Christ is a call to peace and brotherhood—peace and self-control within; kindness, gentleness, courtesy, and consideration to all without. This lesson is too deeply written in the Christian conscience to need further treatment. We call our Lord the "Prince of Peace."

The last clause in this rule, the haggling over prices or driving for a close bargain in buying or selling, is aimed at the selfishness of the sharp trader. Those who use many words in buying or selling are not so anxious to arrive at a just price as to overcome the other party by superior mental adroitness or pressure. What the Christian must seek is fairness in all such dealings—fairness for himself, fairness for the other party.

RULE SIX

[Against] the buying or selling goods that have not paid the duty

SCRIPTURAL BASIS: "Provide things honest in the sight of all men." (Rom. 12:17.) "Render therefore unto Caesar the things which are Caesar's." (Matt. 22:21.) "Render therefore to all their dues." (Rom. 13:7.)

At the time these rules were written, the levying of duty on imported goods was something comparatively new. English people, who traditionally were used to free trade, bitterly resented the idea that the government should tax any of their possessions which they brought into their country. But now it is universally conceded that the government has a right to levy tariffs on imports, and good citizens recognize this everywhere. Every smuggler robs his country and stands as a thief before Almighty God. So do those who defraud their nation by cheating it of its rightful taxes, making fraudulent returns to the income-tax office, and so on. One has no more right to rob the government—or a city or a corporation, for that matter— than to rob a private individual.

RULE SEVEN

[Against] the giving or taking of things on usury —that is, unlawful interest

SCRIPTURAL BASIS: "Lord, who shall abide in thy tabernacle?—who shall dwell in thy holy hill? . . . He that putteth not out his money to usury, nor taketh reward against the innocent." (Ps. 15:1, 5.) "That no man go beyond and defraud his brother." (I Thess. 4:6.)

The Hebrew and Christian view that prevailed for many centuries was that any interest charged for the use of money was "usury" and wrong. But in the clearer view that came with the awakening of the modern world and the necessary expansion of trade and credit, it was seen that the rent of money (interest), like the rent of land or of houses, could be charged properly and accepted, provided such interest was fair and there was no taking advantage of the oppressed.

Wesley, in writing this rule, explained usury as "unlawful interest." The practice forbidden is to receive more for a loan than such loan is worth, measured not only by the law of the land, but by the higher law of the Golden Rule.

RULE EIGHT

[Against] uncharitable or unprofitable conversation; particularly speaking evil of magistrates or ministers

The Bible truly says the "tongue is a fire." More harm is done by idle talking than this world dreams of. Even greater harm is done by speaking evil of persons when they are not present to defend themselves, or by innuendoes which besmudge character. A famous authority once observed that the talebearer and the listener to such tales should both be hanged—one by the tongue, the other by the ear.

RULE NINE

[Against] doing to others as we would not they should do unto us

This really is a negative statement of the Golden Rule and speaks for itself.

RULE TEN

[Against] doing what we know is not for the glory of God, as: the putting on of gold and costly apparel

SCRIPTURAL BASIS: "Whose adorning let it not be that outward adorning of plaiting the hair, and of wearing of gold, or of putting on of apparel." (I Pet. 3:3.) "I will . . . that women adorn themselves in modest apparel, . . . not with braided hair, or gold, or pearls, or costly array." (I Tim. 2:8, 9.)

Needless extravagance in dress and useless and showy ornamentation are forbidden by this rule. It was written in a day when English class distinctions were clear-cut and deep. Those who were then known as "gentlemen" or "ladies" had to dress in a certain fine way in keeping with their station. The common people—and into this class most Methodists belonged—were not expected to put on fine garments, for to do so was considered pretense and hypocrisy. John Wesley energetically forbade his people to "ape the gentleman," as he expressed it.

Christians today do not consider quiet adornment as wrong. Nevertheless, while we have departed somewhat from the strict plainness of early days, it still is true that Christian people have no right to spend on ornaments and unnecessary luxuries anything more than a modest fraction of their means. We could do with much more self-denial today. As long as there are poverty and hunger in the world, as long as there are those in desperate need, we have no right to spend too much upon ourselves. "You are not to adorn yourselves on the outside with braids of hair and ornaments of gold"—so Moffatt translates the verse from I Peter which was given above. To this Goodspeed adds, "Yours must be the inner beauty of character."

RULE ELEVEN

[Against] the taking of such diversions as cannot be used in the name of the Lord Jesus

SCRIPTURAL BASIS: "Be not conformed to this world." (Rom. 12:2.) "Know ye not that the friendship of the world is enmity with God?" (Jas. 4:4.) "Love not the world, neither the things that are in the world." (I John 2:15.)

It is to be noticed that this rule does not cite the diversions which are forbidden. Time after time in the life of the Church various popular amusements have been blacklisted. For a long time the dance, the theater, the circus, were named as worldly amusements unfit for Christian participation. But Christian liberty allows each individual to determine in the sight of God what is right for him. Wholesome recreation has a part in life, and there are many amusements which not only are innocent in themselves, but build up character and refit one for the daily task. But whatever one feels to be wrong for him to do, *to him that particular thing is wrong.*

RULE TWELVE

[Against] the singing those songs, or reading those books which do not tend to the knowledge or love of God

SCRIPTURAL BASIS: "Be not deceived: evil communications corrupt good manners." (I Cor. 15:33.) "Speaking to yourselves in psalms and hymns and spiritual songs, singing and making melody in your heart to the Lord." (Eph. 5:19.) "I count all things but loss for the excellency of the knowledge of Christ Jesus my Lord." (Phil. 3:8.) "And whatsoever ye do in word or deed, do all in the name of the Lord Jesus." (Col. 3:17.)

This rule sets one on the positive way to righteousness by blocking out everything which does not help along that way. It was written to make all time count for God and strictly interpreted would forbid all secular reading and music. Certainly the enjoyment of song and the reading of books which are not harmful in themselves have both recreational and character-building value. On the other hand there are books, plays, and pictures that are definitely harmful. Between these extremes there is the middle register of amusements that are neither very edifying nor positively harmful. Each Christian must decide for himself how much God-given time he shall draw upon for such diversions. All of life must be made to count for righteousness.

RULE THIRTEEN

[Against] softness and needless self-indulgence

SCRIPTURAL BASIS: "Then said Jesus unto his disciples, If any man will come after me, let him deny himself, and take up his cross, and follow me." (Matt. 16:24.)

Self-control, self-denial—these are familiar words in the Christian vocabualry. If athletes, such as prizefighters and distance runners, submit to rigorous training to obtain the fading laurels of earthly victory, surely the people of God can put away ease and self-indulgence and grow in moral stamina as well as grace. "God give us a hardened soldiery," an old Methodist bishop prayed once as he ordained his preachers. No ease-loving people, comfortable and well fixed, can impress the world. "Except I shall see in his hands the print of the nails," said Thomas, "I will not believe."

People would believe our witness more today if we denied ourselves more, gave more, and so appeared to be more in earnest. We cannot spend vast sums upon our homes, our travel, our comfort, our ease in life, without losing something in our own character, as well as a great opportunity to influence the characters of others.

RULE FOURTEEN

[Against] laying up treasure upon earth

SCRIPTURAL BASIS: "Lay not up for yourselves treasures upon earth, where moth and rust doth corrupt, and where thieves break through and steal: but lay up for yourselves treasures in heaven, where neither moth nor rust doth corrupt, and where thieves do not break through nor steal: for where your treasure is, there will your heart be also." (Matt. 6:19-21.)

The positive side of this injunction—to lay up treasures in heaven—could be emphasized even more than the negative. There is no wrong in providing for oneself and one's own in all needful things. Every Christian is expected to pull his own weight in making a living and have something left over, if possible, to pull the weight of others. Paul declared that if a man did not provide for his own and especially for those of his own household, he is "worse than an infidel" (I Tim. 5:8).

Christianity always has taught diligence, thrift, frugality, and that the laborer is worthy of his hire. But earthly values are never to supplant the coinage of heaven. Wesley's rule for managing money is to be remembered: "Make all you can; save all you can; give all you can." Every Christian has been entrusted with earthly goods in order that he may use them for heavenly purposes. It is possible to deal so in earthly treasures as to receive heavenly dividends.

RULE FIFTEEN

[Against] borrowing without a probability of paying; or taking up goods without a probability of paying for them

SCRIPTURAL BASIS: "The wicked borroweth, and payeth not again." (Ps. 37:21.) "Render unto all their dues." (Rom. 18:7.) "Recompense to no man evil for evil. Provide things honest in the sight of all men." (Rom. 12:17.) "Owe no man any thing, but to love one another." (Rom. 13:8.)

Taking chances in matters of financial outlay is forbidden by a common-sense Christianity. To be sure, misfortune in business sometimes overtakes a good man as well as a bad one, and there is risk in all enterprise; but the hasty assumption of heavy obligations, or reckless borrowing, is wrong in the sight of both man and God.

Up to this point we have been following the negative injunctions of the General Rules—what we must *not* do. We now come to the positive rules.

The Positive Rules

"It is expected of all who continue in these societies that they shall continue to evidence their desire of salvation":

RULE SIXTEEN

By doing good; by being in every kind merciful after their power; as they have opportunity, doing good of every possible sort, and, as far as possible, to all men

SCRIPTURAL BASIS: "Trust in the Lord, and do good." (Ps. 37:3.) "To do good and to communicate forget not." (Heb. 13:16.) "Blessed are the merciful: for they shall obtain mercy." (Matt. 5:7.) "To him that knoweth to do good, and doeth it not, to him it is sin." (Jas. 4:17.) "As we have therefore opportunity, let us do good unto all men." (Gal. 6:10.)

85

This is the broad injunction which everyone with the desire to lead a Christian life should have continually before him. Opportunities are open to us on all sides for the doing of good—to ourselves, to our families, to our fellow men, to the world in which we live. There is no way to outline the myriad series of opportunities which come before us each day, but the alert Christian will be able to discern and take advantage of each one.

When the Lord gave his picture of the final judgment, he made his commendation, as well as his condemnation, to depend upon the feeding of the hungry, the visiting of the sick and those in prison, and the doing of good to needy people. "Inasmuch as ye have done it unto one of the least of these my brethren, ye have done it unto me."

The whole matter of kindliness and of Christian charity was thus forever laid upon the hearts of God's people. What is to be remembered is not so much that we must have a sincere intent to do good deeds, but that we shall actually (1) see opportunities and (2) follow them out in acts of service that benefit our fellow men.

RULE SEVENTEEN

[Doing good] to their bodies, of the ability of which God giveth, by giving food to the hungry, by clothing the naked, by visiting or helping them that are sick or in prison

SCRIPTURAL BASIS: "Then shall the King say unto them on his right hand, Come, ye blessed of my Father, inherit the kingdom prepared for you from the foundation of the world: for I was an hungred, and ye gave me meat: I was thirsty, and ye gave me drink: I was a stranger, and ye took me in: naked, and ye clothed me: I was sick, and ye visited me: I was in prison, and ye came unto me. . . . Inasmuch as ye have done it unto one of the least of these my brethren, ye have done it unto me." (Matt. 25:34-36, 40.)

RULE EIGHTEEN

[Doing good] to their souls, by instructing, reproving or exhorting all we have any intercourse with; trampling

86

under foot that enthusiastic doctrine, that "we are not to do good unless our hearts be free to it."

SCRIPTURAL BASIS: "Reprove, rebuke, exhort with all longsuffering and doctrine." (II Tim. 4:2.) "Exhort one another daily." (Heb. 3:13.) "Them that sin rebuke before all, that others also may fear." (I Tim. 5:20).) "Ye are the salt of the earth . . . ye are the light of the world." (Matt. 5:13, 14.)

The two rules above are so obvious that they need only to be put down to be approved. To do good to the bodies and souls of men—this has been the law of Christianity ever since Jesus, the great physician, sent his disciples out to teach and to heal. In a world where the have-nots outnumber the haves, where there is a desperate need on every side, the ancient command to "do good unto all men" is never to be forgotten. "No man hungers but that I hunger; no man thirsts but that I thirst." This is the true Christian attitude.

The United Methodist passion for social justice, so strong today, stems directly from the principle laid down in these rules. United Methodism is not, and never has been, the private cultivation of a mere inner spirituality. Rather it is the dynamic outgrowing of the Christian spirit into every area of life where good can be done to the souls and bodies of men. Its aggressive attack upon evil, public and private, caused one writer to describe Methodism as an "invasive encampment upon the field of the world."

A word of explanation is due here regarding the last expression of Rule Eighteen: "trampling under foot that enthusiastic doctrine . . . not to do good unless our hearts be free to it." Certain sincere, but unrealistic, Christians at the time of John Wesley taught that if one did not feel like doing a good deed, it was wrong for him to make any move to do it. They refused to partake of the sacrament unless they felt that they were perfectly prepared, and even believed it wrong to pray unless moved to it.

Wesley and the early Methodists repudiated these strange ideas with all the force they had. Wesley said that when one did not feel like going to church or taking Communion or praying, that was the very time when he should do these

87

things. Christianity always moves forward by "trampling under foot" any feelings which interfere with duty. We are to be guided not by our immediate impulses, but by what we know to be right.

RULE NINETEEN

By doing good, especially to them that are of the household of faith or groaning so to be; employing them preferably to others; buying one of another; helping each other in business; and so much the more because the world will love its own and them *only*

SCRIPTURAL BASIS: "As we have therefore opportunity, let us do good unto all men, especially unto them who are of the household of faith." (Gal. 6:10.) "Be kindly affectioned one to another with brotherly love; in honour preferring one another; . . . distributing to the necessity of saints; given to hospitality." (Rom. 12:10, 13.)

Christian fellowship and mutual helpfulness are taught all through the Bible. Every Christian group is expected to be a brotherhood, and the Church itself has sometimes been called the "communion of the saints."

In the New Testament the Church is regarded as a family—the "household of God." Such a household must have affection to bind the family circle together, obedience holding all to the rules of the home, and a loving attitude tying brother to brother and sister to sister.

In a practical way this rule stresses the duty of Christians to stand by one another in the economic and social undertakings of life. Where a brother churchman has a store or conducts a business, we should buy from him and patronize those who belong to our fellowship. To be sure, the Christian brotherhood is not a partnership for economic and social profit, although there are persons who join the church in order to gain temporally. Jesus himself had some who followed him for the "loaves and the fishes." But as the rule here reminds us, the "world will love its own" (worldly people stick together), and so should Christians. "We are a colony of heaven." Paul beautifully expressed it (Phil. 3:20 Moffatt).

RULE TWENTY

[Shall so live] by all possible diligence and frugality that the gospel be not blamed

SCRIPTURAL BASIS: "Not slothful in business; fervent in spirit; serving the Lord." (Rom. 12:11.) "If any provide not for his own, and specially for those of his own house, he hath denied the faith, and is worse than an infidel." (I Tim. 5:8.)

This rule is simple—likewise direct. Diligence means care and attention to details, and an earnest busyness about the affairs of life; frugality means saving ("making it do"), and this not wholly for ourselves but to have more for all.

Every Christian is therefore expected (as was said of Rule Fourteen), to pull his own weight in the world and then to help others pull theirs. The Bible has no patience with economic parasites, or those who try to get without giving. In a day when the idea has grown that people are to be taken care of by the government or by a collectivist society, the robust idea of this rule (which was also that of our early American forebears) is to be remembered. "If any provide not for his own, . . . he hath denied the faith."

RULE TWENTY-ONE

[Shall live] by running with patience the race that is set before them, denying themselves, and taking up their cross daily, submitting to bear the reproach of Christ, to be as the filth and offscouring of the world; and looking that men should say all manner of evil of them falsely, for the Lord's sake

SCRIPTURAL BASIS: "Seeing we also are compassed about with so great a cloud of witnesses, let us lay aside every weight, and the sin which doth so easily beset us, and let us run with patience the race that is set before us." (Heb. 12:1.) "If any man will come after me, let him deny himself, and take up his cross, and follow me." (Matt. 16:24.) "We are made as the filth of the world, and are the offscouring of all things unto this day." (I Cor. 4:13.) "Blessed are ye, when men shall revile you, and persecute you, and shall say all manner of evil against you falsely, for my sake." (Matt. 5:11.)

89

This rule requires the cultivation of patience, a virtue which is not easy to come by. It sets the pace not for a quick race, but for enduring whatever life has to bring. Our business in life is to grow in grace as followers of the Lord. To do so we must not only have patience but be ready to endure sorrow, expect opposition, and, if need be, accept poverty and the reverses of fortune. In every life there is a cross which must be taken up daily. God has not promised us happiness, but he has promised us the peace which passeth all understanding—the deep assurance that whatever happens, his goodness and mercy are over all his children.

The third division of the General Rules outlines positive religious duties.

Positive Religious Duties

At this point comes in the churchliness of United Methodism. Up to now the rules laid down might be taken by any pious person or sectarian group as proper guidance on what to do and what not to do. But the General Rules were not given simply to guide a "society" but members of the Church of God —the Church with its preaching, its sacraments, its ordered ministries. The rules that here follow are a direct contradiction to the idea that Methodism is simply a set of pious, personal regulations. Over all its doctrine, organization, and discipline is The Church—holy, catholic, eternal—in which every United Methodist must have his being if he is to be a United Methodist at all.

"It is expected of all who desire to continue in these societies that they shall continue to evidence their desire of salvation":

RULE TWENTY-TWO

By attending upon all the ordinances of God; such [as] the public worship of God

SCRIPTURAL BASIS: "One thing have I desired of the Lord, that will I seek after; that I may dwell in the house of the Lord all the days of my life, to behold the beauty of the Lord, and to enquire

90

in his temple." (Ps. 27:4.) "Not forsaking the assembling of ourselves together, as the manner of some is." (Heb. 10:25.)

RULE TWENTY-THREE

[Should attend] the ministry of the Word, either read or expounded

SCRIPTURAL BASIS: Christ instituted his ministry and said, "Go ye
therefore, and teach all nations, . . . teaching them to observe all
things whatsoever I have commanded you: and, lo, I am with you
alway even unto the end of the world." (Matt. 28:19, 20.) "So
then faith cometh by hearing, and hearing by the word of God."
(Rom. 10:17.) "But whoso looketh into the perfect law of liberty,
and continueth therein, he being not a forgetful hearer, but a doer
of the work, this man shall be blessed in his deed." (Jas. 1:25.)

These two rules naturally belong together, for one is the
extension of the other. Christians must attend public worship for their souls' health. It refits them for life, feeds them
spiritually, and is the God-given method whereby the Church
holds and nurtures its own. Absence from public worship
represents a spiritual loss, and willful and continued absence
always ends with a *forgotten Church and a forgotten God.*
Every United Methodist should attend church when services
are held in his church on Sunday, and every pastor who fails
to remind his people of this, their duty, is remiss in his.

Church attendance is not intended to be a spectator sport
in which passive worshipers hear the delivery of a sermon and
watch a paid choir conduct music. Participation on the part
of each is more than duty; it becomes a genuine gladness when
entered into sincerely. The responsive readings, the unison
prayers, and especially the hymns of the church—in these our
people are expected to participate and are glad to do so.

RULE TWENTY-FOUR

[Must not neglect] the Supper of the Lord

SCRIPTURAL BASIS: (For this and our Church's teachings regarding
the Lord's Supper and its observance, see pages 48, 130.)

The sacrament of the Lord's Supper has always been to every Christian a true means of grace. God's table is set and ready. His people must "draw near with faith"; and when they do, they literally take the sacrament, as our ritual has it, "to [their] comfort." (For a more complete discussion, pages 130-36.)

RULE TWENTY-FIVE

[Must not neglect] family and private prayer

SCRIPTURAL BASIS: "As for me and my house, we will serve the Lord." (Josh. 24:15.) "When thou prayest, enter into thy closet, and when thou hast shut thy door, pray to thy Father which is in secret; and thy Father which seest in secret shall reward thee openly." (Matt. 6:6.) "Pray without ceasing. In every thing give thanks." (I Thess. 5:17-18.)

The old custom of holding family prayers has been discarded in most modern United Methodist homes, and the loss is very great. Many a man or woman living today in the fullness of Christian maturity looks back with gratitude to family prayers in his own home. Just as every child has the right to be wellborn, so every child should have the right to be surrounded continually by Christian influences—by grace at the table and a brief period of home devotion. Admittedly it is difficult to find the time for this stated prayer in a home today, but it can be done and means much in Christian life. Short scripture reading and prayer at the breakfast hour is the way many United Methodist families manage this.

The Bible has much to say about praying in solitude, and our Lord himself set an example here. If Jesus found it necessary to pray, his disciples surely need it far more. Much is heard today about peace of mind and peace of soul, but the peace that the gospel knows is that inner spiritual assurance that always comes to those who make their way regularly into the secret of God's presence by meditation and prayer. No matter how busy the schedule or how rushed the life, time must be taken for this.

RULE TWENTY-SIX

[Must not neglect] searching the Scriptures

SCRIPTURAL BASIS: "I will meditate in thy precepts, and have respect unto thy ways. I will delight myself in thy statutes: I will not forget thy word." (Ps. 119:15-16.) "Search the scriptures; for in them ye think ye have eternal life: and they are they which testify of me." (John 5:39.)

There is a personal message in the Book of God which speaks directly to the heart of every man. Against all doubters the Bible is its own best witness. Truth has a self-evidencing power nowhere stronger felt than when the pages of sacred writ are studied and read. There are today excellent commentaries and a wealth of reverent interpretations which help us to understand the truth of God's Word. These echo the words of the psalmist: "Send out thy light and thy truth: let them lead me; let them bring me unto thy holy hill" (Ps. 43:3).

"The Bible is a rock of diamonds, a chain of pearls, the sword of the Spirit," said Dr. Watson; "a chart by which the Christian sails to eternity; the map by which he daily walks; the sun-dial by which he sets his life; the balances in which he weighs his action."

It has been said that no one can live in sin and read the Bible ten minutes every day. One action blocks out the other. Let God's people read continually the sacred Book, and it truly will be a "lamp unto [their] feet," opening more and more into the light of the perfect day.

RULE TWENTY-SEVEN

[Must not neglect] fasting or abstinence

SCRIPTURAL BASIS: Fasting has been a method of religious observance throughout the ages. It was prescribed in the Old Testament; it was observed in the New. "As they ministered to the Lord, and fasted, the Holy Ghost said, Separate me Barnabas and Saul for the work whereunto I have called them. And when they had fasted and prayed, and laid their hands on them, they sent them away." (Acts 13:2-3.) "And when they had ordained them elders in every church, and had prayed with fasting, they commended them to the Lord, on whom they believed." (Acts 14:23.)

We do not put as much emphasis upon the need of fasting as did our fathers. The old theory was that it was spiritually healthy to mortify, that is, to kill, the impulses of the body. Modern Christians are inclined to believe that the needs of the body should neither obtrude themselves unduly nor be crushed unduly. For many people there is a spiritual value in abstaining from food at certain times; for others there is the feeling that since abstention from food is a break in the ordered regimen of the day, thus slackening efficiency by that much, it need not be insisted upon so strongly.

Nevertheless, just as when we are under some high emotional strain, as in danger or in great sorrow, and we do not feel like touching food, so when we desire earnestly to find our way into some great spiritual experience, we can wisely push from us the satisfaction of material wants. Concerning fasting, let each one be fully persuaded in his own mind. We appreciate the fact that occasionally in our nation's history, national as well as church leaders have called for days of fasting and prayer, that all may take occasion to think more deeply upon eternal verities.

John Wesley ended the General Rules with an impressive statement given here in its entirety:

These are the General Rules of our societies; all of which we are taught of God to observe, even in his written Word, which is the only rule, and the sufficient rule, both of our faith and practice. And all these we know his Spirit writes on truly awakened hearts. If there be any among us who observe them not, who habitually breaks any of them, let it be known unto them who watch over that soul as they who must give an account. We will admonish him of the error of his ways. We will bear with him for a season. But, if then he repent not, he hath no more place among us. We have delivered our own souls.

So John Wesley closed the rules of the Methodist canon.

CHAPTER FIVE

Organization

To each United Methodist lay person the organization of his own local church seems more important than the big over-all structure of United Methodism as a whole. This is under-standable. He lives his life in the local church, attends its services, contributes to its finances, and if he is a member of the Administrative Board has a direct part to play in its work. He knows in a general way that The United Methodist Church is a big institution with bishops and boards, conferences and huge budgets. But too often the average layperson feels that the United Methodist organization is too complicated for him to understand; and as he does not necessarily have to under-stand it, he is inclined to dismiss it from further thought. But this is neither sensible nor correct. It is not too difficult to understand the United Methodist organization, and every United Methodist should know in a general way how it func-tions.

It functions through bishops, district superintendents, preachers-in-charge, Board secretaries, and local church officials who may be called Executive Officers; also through a chain of conferences—General Conference, Jurisdictional Conference, Annual Conference, District Conference, Charge Conference, and Church Conference—which may be termed Legislative or Administrative Bodies; and also through the regulations and provisions of the *Book of Discipline* which in addition to outlining the rights and duties of the executive and legislative bodies of the Church, provides a body of trial and administrative law which heads up in the Judicial Council or "Supreme Court" of the Church.

The United Methodist Church, though large, is a closely knit organization. The unit of the organization is the local church, or "charge," as it is technically called in Methodism. A charge may be one or more local churches. If it is one church, it is a "station charge," or "station": if more than one church, the group is a "circuit" and is called a "circuit charge."

Charges are grouped geographically into "districts," each supervised by a minister known as the district superintendent.

Districts in turn compose a larger grouping, the Annual Conference. This is presided over by a bishop.

Annual Conferences make up larger regional divisions known as jurisdictions, of which there are five in the United States. Outside the United States Annual Conferences are grouped into what are called Central Conferences.

The General Conference

This is the supreme governing and lawmaking body of United Methodism and one of the most influential church bodies in the world. It meets every four years and directs the affairs of the church. It is composed of ministers and laymen in equal numbers, all of whom are elected as delegates by the Annual Conferences.

Every Annual Conference is allowed to elect ministerial and lay delegates in equal numbers, ministerial members electing ministerial delegates, laypersons electing lay delegates. The General Conference itself, under the Constitution of the Church, has the right to determine how many delegates each annual conference may elect proportionate to the size of each Annual Conference.

No one can belong to the General Conference unless elected to it by one of the Annual Conferences of United Methodism. There are no appointive or *ex-officio* members. The bishops preside over the General Conference but are not members of it. Of recent years the Methodist Church of Great Britain has been allowed to send and seat four delegates in it.

As the Evangelical United Brethren Church was quite a bit smaller than The Methodist Church at the time of union in 1968, it was agreed and written into the constitution of The United Methodist Church, that the E.U.B. conferences and membership should have for the first twelve years after union a larger proportion of representation in the General Conference and in certain important bodies of the new church, than would be prescribed for the regular Methodist Conferences and membership.

The business of the General Conference is to revise the *Discipline*, make laws, and determine all sorts of important matters having to do with the ongoing of the Church. At its opening session it first hears a comprehensive report from all the bishops—the "Episcopal Address." This address may be likened to the President's message to each new Congress on the state of the nation. The General Conference then proceeds to do its work by repealing or amending old laws, by passing new ones, and by determining the course of the Church for the next four years.

It has full powers to:

1. Define and fix the powers of Annual Conferences, Mission Conferences, District and Quarterly Conferences, and smaller church bodies.

2. Define and fix the powers of the bishops, ministers, and church members where these have not already been determined by the Constitution of the Church.

3. Revise the hymnbook and ritual of the church when necessary and provide forms for worship in accordance with United Methodist usage and custom.

4. Plan and in large measure direct all the connectional enterprises, such as missions, education, publishing interests, hospitals, ministerial training, and the like.

5. Set up a budget for the whole church for the coming four years and determine how this is to be raised and administered.

The General Conference has sweeping powers to "enact such other legislation as may be necessary, subject to the limitations and restrictions of the Constitution of the Church."

97

There are some things the General Conference cannot do:

1. Change the Articles of Religion, the Confession of Faith, or the standards of Methodist doctrine.

2. Destroy the episcopacy (administration by bishops).

3. Change the General Rules of the Church.

4. Do away with the privileges of a church trial as prescribed in the *Discipline*.

5. Appropriate the produce of the Publishing House for any other cause than the support of the retired preachers and the widows and orphans of preachers.

6. Elect bishops, as bishops are now elected by the Jurisdictional Conferences.

7. Change the Constitution of The United Methodist Church, though it can *recommend* a change by a two-thirds vote. Such a change to be effected will then require the consent of two-thirds of the members of all the Annual Conferences who shall later vote, conference by conference. It would require three-fourths of such Conference membership present and voting, to change an Article of Religion or Confession of Faith.

The Jurisdictional Conference

At the time of church union in 1939 the Methodist Church inside the United States was divided for administrative purposes into regions known as jurisdictions. Five of these were geographic, and one was racial, this last, which has now been absorbed by the others, was composed of the black conferences which had been a part of the former Methodist Episcopal Church.

The five geographic jurisdictions, continued in The United Methodist Church, are as follows: The North Central, the Northeastern, the South Central, the Southeastern, and the Western. Each of these covers a certain large section of the United States and unites the Annual Conferences of that section into a jurisdiction. For some years the Negro Annual Conferences were grouped together to form a jurisdiction of their own known as the Central Jurisdiction. The United Methodist Church in 1968 made no provision for such a racially distinguished jurisdiction, and the black Annual Conferences were thereafter merged into their overarching Annual Conferences of the other jurisdictions.

The Jurisdictional Conferences meet once every four years, all at the same time, which time is determined by the Council of Bishops. Usually this is within a month or two after the meeting of the General Conference. Each Jurisdictional Conference is composed of the elected representatives of the Annual Conferences who have been members of the General Conference immediately preceding; plus a proportionate number of additional ministers and laymen elected according to a ratio determined by the General Conference. This gives equitable representation to all Annual Conferences in accord with their size and membership. Ministers and lay persons must be elected in equal numbers to both the General and Jurisdictional Conferences.

The great duty of the Jurisdictional Conference is to elect bishops and the members of most of the boards and general agencies of the church. It must also plan the general program of church work to be carried out within the jurisdiction during the coming four years.

The number of bishops to be elected by the respective Jurisdictional Conferences depends upon the number of church members enrolled in the jurisdiction. Every jurisdiction having 500,000 church members is allowed to have six bishops and for each additional 500,000 church members or major fraction thereof any jurisdiction shall be entitled to elect one additional bishop.

An exception is made in the case of those jurisdictions where there may be more than 70,000 square miles in each episcopal area as an average. Such jurisdictions are allowed to have six bishops for the first 400,000 members and one additional bishop for each additional 400,000, or two-thirds thereof. The Western Jurisdiction comes under this exception.

The election of bishops and board members is vested in the Jurisdictional Conference in order that the different sections of the country may have proportionate representation upon all the boards and in the bishopric.

Central Conferences

Central Conferences are in effect Jurisdictional Conferences outside the United States and its territories. The Annual Conferences in a certain land or region, as for instance northern Europe or Southern Asia, meet each four years in a Central Conference, as it is called. Such conferences have important powers of election and direction with regard to their own affairs. They elect bishops in the number determined by the General Conference and sometimes elect them for a term of years rather than for life as are bishops of the five jurisdictions. Central Conference bishops, however, have all the powers of the traditional Methodist episcopacy in almost every essential.

The Annual Conference

The Annual Conference is the basic body of United Methodism. It consists of all the traveling preachers who live within a certain territory and of lay members, duly elected.

Ministers when once admitted to an Annual Conference become members of it for life, unless they withdraw or are "located" or expelled. They are known as "traveling preachers." Every ministerial member of the conference must receive an annual appointment by the Bishop unless he has been formally retired. Ministers can be transferred (moved from one Annual Conference to another) but no minister can be refused an appointment as long as he is a member of an Annual Conference.

An Annual Conference can "locate" a ministerial member by formal vote when he does not impress the conference as being suitable or qualified for the traveling ministry. This makes him a lay pastor again. A minister may locate voluntarily by requesting that he be allowed to drop out of the itinerant, or traveling, ministry and resume the status of a lay pastor. The Conference has to vote each "location."

The lay members of the Annual Conference are elected by their local churches. Each charge is allowed to elect one lay delegate only, unless the charge—usually a large one—has more than one minister. In such case the charge may be allowed to elect lay delegates equal to the number of ministers assigned to such charge. A new provision recently adopted now calls for as many lay members in the annual conference as there are ministerial members. (See page 147.)

The Annual Conference has very important powers:

1. To determine what ministers shall be admitted to its membership, ordained, retired, located, or granted special leave.

2. To vote on all constitutional amendments as these may be proposed by the General Conference.

3. To elect delegates to the General and Jurisdictional Conferences once every four years.

4. To have all other rights which have not been delegated to the General Conference under the constitution.

This last is extremely important. It keeps all reserved powers in the hands of the Annual Conferences rather than in the hands of the General Conference, as was the case before church union in 1939.

A bishop presides over each session of the Annual Conference; and when acting in this capacity, he is termed the "conference president." He must see that the business of the conference is properly managed and that the age-old United Methodist Annual Conference questions—some of them out of the old *General Minutes* of Wesley's first conferences—are asked and answered.

The Annual Conference, although it has a lay member from each charge, is historically a preachers' conference. Its chief duties have to do with the ministry and its work—with ministers' reports, ministers' characters, ministers' superannuation, ministers' admission on trial, ministers' ordination, and the stationing of the ministers (the "appointments").

To be sure there are other matters of high import which each Annual Conference must act upon, and the lay members have an important part to play. They participate in all deliberations and vote upon all measures except on the granting or validation of license, ordination, reception into full membership, or any question concerning the character and official conduct of ministers. There are many committees to report, many plans made for work during the year, many causes and interests to be looked after.

Membership in an Annual Conference is considered a high privilege and rightly so. Conferences take pride in their accomplishments and personnel and vie with one another in the work of United Methodism. Every Annual Conference is governed by the same rules and conducts its business in the same way as every other Annual Conference, but there are characteristic differences which give to each a certain individuality.

The actions and influence of a United Methodist Annual Conference have great weight in its own region. Other Christian denominations are influenced by "what the Methodists do," and the social and political life of a whole state feels the impact of the United Methodist conference.

The District Conference

A District Conference is held once a year in every district superintendent's area if the Annual Conference containing that district so orders. If an Annual Conference decides not to have District Conferences, none are held; if it decides to have District Conferences, these are held year after year in all the districts of that particular Annual Conference.

The District Conference when it is held consists of all the preachers who are serving charges in the district, together with all local preachers, and a certain number of lay delegates elected from each charge as well as certain district officers. It is presided over by the district superintendent, who is expected to take the occasion to check up on the progress of the work in his district and to see that the program of the church is properly presented and supported. The various causes of the general church are represented at the District Conference, often by visiting general church officials who are thus enabled to give the District Conference a view of the progress and purposes of the church's work.

The Charge Conference

We now come to that part of the Methodist organization which is of special importance to members of the local church

—their Charge Conference, known all throughout Methodist history until 1968 as the Quarterly Conference.

The Charge Conference is the governing body of the local church or charge. Belonging to it are all the officials of the local church—the pastor, assistant pastors if any, members of the Administrative Board, trustees, local preachers if any, superintendent of the church school, the president of the local United Methodist Women, and a number of other specified officers as listed in the *Book of Discipline*.

The Charge Conference must meet once each year and may meet at such other times as may be necessary. One meeting is absolutely essential in order to elect church officers for the next year, determine the salary of the minister, and take other essential actions.

Presiding over the Charge Conference is the district superintendent.[3] At its sessions he asks for regular reports from the pastor and from the other officials and committees of the charge. The *Discipline* directs the district superintendent as to what questions he must ask and what reports he must call for. This is a uniform procedure over all United Methodism, so that not only is the business of each local church reviewed and brought up to date at charge conference time, but it is done the same way in every United Methodist church. The questions asked in Tennessee at the Charge Conference are the same questions asked in the Charge Conference in Montana or in southern Texas or anywhere else. The Charge Conference is the connecting link between the local church and all United Methodism.

The Charge Conference has important *executive* powers. It decides what the pastor's salary shall be, what amount of money it shall accept as its share of general church work, and how the business affairs of the local church are to be managed. It can buy or build, sell or mortgage a church building or parsonage, and in general takes care of all property matters according to the *Discipline* of the Church and the laws of the respective states.

Formerly the Quarterly Conference (as it was then called)

[3] The office of district superintendent is discussed on page 116.

of the charge—which might be composed of several circuit churches—managed the property of each one of its local churches. This caused difficulties, and in 1952 it was provided that each local church on a circuit, no matter how small, must have its own Church Quarterly Conference to take care of its special property rights. This plan has largely been continued in the present United Methodist Church through separate Charge Conferences.

Certain important commissions and committees are set up by the Charge Conference to assist in carrying on its work. Such commissions have been known by different names as successive General Conferences have recast them from time to time, but each deals with matters essential to local church administration. Foremost among them are: the Committee on Nominations and Personnel; that on Pastor-Parish Relations; and that on Finance. There is also a new and powerful body known as the Council on Ministries in each local church which has the responsibility for overseeing the general administrative work of the church in many important ways.

The Committee on Nominations and Personnel is very important since it proposes to the Charge Conference, usually at its final meeting of the year, those who are to be elected officials of the local church for the ensuing year. Recent regulations have required that this committee be composed of not more than nine persons beside the pastor who must always serve as its chairman. It nominates to the Charge Conference, with the district superintendent presiding, such officers and members of the Administrative Board and Charge Conference and committees as may be required.

In early Methodism the pastor alone named the stewards and trustees, but in time the Quarterly Conference, as it was then known, took this over, though the pastor until recent years continued to make all nominations. Today the pastor is made chairman of the committee to make the nominations. However, when this committee itself is to be elected by the Charge Conference, nominations from the floor are to be called for. Criticism is sometimes heard that the Charge Conference is a self-perpetuating group which continues to "run" the local church, with their own nominating committee continuing to nominate themselves year after year. A wise committee on nominations, and a wise pastor, will see to it that representative persons from different groups in the church will be put forward by the Committee on Nominations and Personnel. This will broaden the base and increase the efficiency of the entire body.

The Committee on Pastor-Parish Relations has to do with the important matter of aiding the pastor and his staff "in making his ministry effective by being available for counsel, keeping him advised concerning conditions within the congregation as they affect relations between pastor and people, and continually interpreting to the people the nature and function of the pastoral office." If for any reason a change of pastors is being comtemplated, the work of this committee is very important. It acts as a consultative agency for the church. Such a committee is forbidden by the *Discipline* to have a private meeting unless the minister or district superintendent shall be informed of such a meeting. Good churchmanship calls for all this committee's moves to be open and above board. Normally this committee is expected to be of great help to the pastor when he needs its counseling, and it also has the responsibility for supplying the pulpit temporarily if the pastor should be ill or on vacation. It also has under its purview matters regarding the minister's salary, travel expense, vacation, and the like.

The Committee on Finance, now elected under that name, has always been an extremely important agency in each local church. While the Administrative Board of the church, as we shall show, has today the most to do with church finances, yet such important matters as compiling the budget for the local church, certifying to the district superintendent what the pastor's salary shall be for the next year, and all sorts of plans for implementing and meeting the financial obligations of the local church must be assumed by the Charge Conference.

This Conference has long carried on its detailed administrative work through important "commissions," or as they are presently termed, "work areas" or "work area commissions." The names of these and frequent adjustment of the interlocking responsibilities among them may be expected to be altered as successive General Conferences see fit to make changes. However, always there will be need for a commission (or "work area,") on Education, as this will have to do with church school and church school literature; a commission on evangelism, whose name describes its functions; a commission on missions and missionary activities; a commission on social concerns; one on stewardship; and often one on worship; and a commission on ecumenical or worldwide church affairs. All these have responsibilities in their allotted fields. They function through or in connection with the local church's Council on Ministries, which is in itself an important supervisory administrative agency in each local church and a somewhat new feature in United Methodist organizational work, coming from the Evangelical United Brethren Church.

It will not be possible to outline all the various duties and responsibilities of these and local church committees. As with all United Methodist organizational work, the current *Book of Discipline* must be referred to for immediate regulations affecting local church organization. It is the purpose here to indicate in a general way the manner in which the Charge Conference carries on its work.

The Administrative Board

An Administrative Board formerly known as the Official Board must be organized in every local church in United Methodism. It is composed of the pastor, the trustees, and other members formerly known as stewards who must be nominated by the Committee on Nominations and Personnel. The Board also includes the director of Christian Education, the President of the United Methodist Women, and certain other specified persons. The *Discipline* carefully prescribes all those who shall be members of this Board.

The Administrative Board is the executive agency of the Charge Conference and technically derives its power from that body. Actually, however, the Administrative Board is the real power in every Methodist Church. This is because it meets monthly rather than once or twice a year (as does the Charge Conference); it is tightly organized; it effectively controls all finances; all its members belong to the Charge Conference, and it is in reality the "cabinet" of the pastor, working hand in glove with him at all times.

The Administrative Board and the Charge Conference do not come into conflict since the same people compose both organizations. The Charge Conference is really the Administrative Board meeting with the district superintendent when he comes to oversee the local church's larger connectional responsibilities; the Administrative Board is really the Charge Conference meeting as its own administrative agency.

The great duty of the Administrative Board is to manage church finances and supervise overall administration. The relation of this Board to the committee on finance has already been referred to. Some churches through the Charge Conference simply turn the whole work of finance over to the Administrative Board or direct that the Board itself shall be the committee on finance.

The Administrative Board implementing its effect through the Charge Conference as it usually does must determine:

(1) What the charge shall pay as salary to the minister or ministers, after consultation with the committee on pastor-parish relations and the committee on finance. The salary must be set firmly in advance of every new conference year so that the appointive power may know exactly what the preacher sent there may depend upon.

(2) What shall be the "acceptance" on the part of the local church—that is, what the charge shall raise as its share of the general funds of the church. Local churches have the right to accept, reject, or modify the allotment apportioned their church as its share of such funds, but local churches take pride in doing their full part for United Methodism. The *Discipline* says that the "Administrative Board shall cultivate interest in all the benevolent causes authorized by the General, Jurisdictional, Annual, and District Conferences, and encour-

107

age the support of world service, Conference and other benevolences."

What amount shall be raised in the local church for other purposes and how this shall be expended is of course also the responsibility of the Administrative Board, but it is not necessary that all such plans shall be cleared through the Charge Conference. In all these financial matters, however, everything depends on the energetic and effective work of the men and women of the Administrative Board. No other members of the church feel free to act in place of the Board.

General Church Boards and Agencies

The United Methodist Church creates a number of church-wide "agencies" or general boards and commissions, each designed to carry on some special function of its work. Of recent years there has been considerable restructuring of these general agencies of the Church. It is no part of this book to describe each of these agencies in a particular way. It should be said, however, that each general agency has come into existence to fulfill a positive need. The Board of Missions had to be created to oversee the missionary work of the Church; the Board of Education to supervise the work of the Church in church schools and colleges; the Board of Health and Welfare to oversee the numerous hospitals, orphanages, homes for the aged, and the like, which the Church has. The essential value of these boards and agencies is that they carry on their work continually with a paid staff in their respective headquarters, and while conferences adjourn and Bishops and church executives scatter out into their several places of responsibility the boards keep steadily on, fulfilling day by day their allotted duties.

The following features mark these organizations: (1) Each is created by the General Conference, which prescribes its membership and duties, and provides for its support. (2) Most boards are incorporated so they can hold property and manage their own affairs under the *Discipline*'s direction. (3) Each board and commission has an employed staff with executives, secretaries, headquarters, promotional literature, and so on.

Most Boards are supported by the World Service Fund (page 151) and are quite often referred to as "world service agencies." One exception is the Board of Publication, which manages The United Methodist Publishing House and is self-supporting, devoting its net gains to retired ministers and conference "claimants." It is therefore not considered a world service agency, nor are certain other agencies of a minor character which receive their support from special offerings. Also, United Methodist Women—the successor of the Women's Society of Christian Service—raises its own funds, (page 147.) For a complete study of these several boards and agencies the *Discipline* must be referred to.

The Judicial Council

In closing this chapter, it seems fitting to say something about a unique feature of Methodist organization—the Judicial Council and United Methodist trial law. The United Methodist Church has a complete judicial system outlined in the book of *Discipline*. This provides for the proper trial of church members and of ministers where charges affecting their character or official actions are brought against them in a formal way. It provides also for an appeal when the decisions of trial committees are against them. A Committee on Appeals is created in each jurisdiction in order to pass upon all cases properly referred to it. Its decisions are final.

The church also has as its supreme court a Judicial Council. This body is established by the constitution of the church and has the power to rule upon the constitutionality of any act of the General Conference. It is also the duty of the Council to hear all appeals from a bishop's decision when one is formally made in an Annual Conference and deals with a question of United Methodist law. There is no appeal from the Judicial Council's decision. Its ruling at once establishes firm United Methodist law.

The Judicial Council sits during the sessions of the General

Conference, as well as at other stated times. When the General Conference passes a law which the Judicial Council considers a violation of the constitution of the church, the report of the Judicial Council declaring the measure unconstitutional at once nullifies the law in question. However, the General Conference can pass the measure again by a two-thirds vote and refer it to the Annual Conferences as a proposal to amend the constitution. As was previously stated in the paragraph dealing with constitutional amendments, if two thirds of the members of the Annual Conferences, present and voting, shall then approve the proposal, it will be declared adopted as constitutional law.

CHAPTER SIX

Ministry and Church Officials

The United Methodist Church believes in a "called ministry." That is, it believes that true ministers of Jesus Christ will have a "sense of oughtness" toward the preaching of the gospel, a sense of calling or mission. Therefore the church's process, when it licenses persons to preach, then ordains them and gives them pulpits and pastorates, is motivated by the desire to find out first of all whether or not a man has been truly called of God. "How shall we try those who profess to be moved by the Holy Ghost to preach?" was John Wesley's carefully worded question, rephrased somewhat today in our *Discipline*. Wesley, and the church after him, outlined and put into effect various ways of trying and testing men.

Becoming a Minister

Let us follow the career of a typical United Methodist preacher. A young person feels called to preach. After talking with his/her[1] pastor and district superintendent, if this conviction continues, that person then goes before the Charge Conference for its recommendation for a license to preach. His/her case is stated to the Conference, and usually the pastor or some friend in the Conference seconds his/her request.

[1] As the language of the former *Disciplines* of the Church was considered "male oriented and discriminatory" an amendment to the Constitution of The United Methodist Church now orders that all pronouns indicating the sex of ministers and church officers shall be changed so that no such discrimination shall longer appear. Hence we use the "he/she" formula when referring to ministers in this chapter.

111

A Charge Conference and all the committees and Conferences which subsequently pass on his/her case are expected to be on the lookout for two things: Has he/she *gifts?* Has he/she *grace?* For there are pious Christians who have no gifts for the preaching or pastoral ministry, and on the other hand there occasionally appear very gifted persons who have no deep sense of mission and whose very profession is sometimes suspect.

Assuming however that a Charge Conference recommends a young person for a license to preach, he/she then goes before the District Committee on the Ministry. This is composed of the District Superintendent and five other ministers. If they are favorably impressed by the applicant, they vote to license him/her to preach. This gives him or her a parchment stating that he or she has authority to preach the gospel. Such a person is thereafter expected to preach whenever called upon to do so by his/her pastor or district superintendent. He or she has become a *lay pastor*—traditionally called a *local preacher.*

Such persons are true ministers of the gospel, and United Methodism owes much of its success to them. However, the church is under no obligation to furnish a lay pastor with a pulpit or provide for his support unless he/she goes into the regular work of the ministry and is put in charge of an appointment.

Becoming a lay pastor is for a young person usually the first step toward entering the full-time ministry. United Methodism believes in an educated ministry as well as a called one, and demands of her ministers that they pass through a period of study with collegiate and if possible theological training before they can be accepted for the full-time ministry. Meantime every lay pastor (or local preacher) is expected to preach from time to time as opportunity presents itself or as the over-pastor may request.

Assuming that all necessary training has been completed the candidate in due time comes before the Conference Board of the Ministry asking for admission to the Annual Conference "on trial."

Traveling Preachers

At the Annual Conference the Conference Board of the Ministry examines him/her carefully as to education, fitness for the ministry, Christian intent and experience, and personal gifts and abilities. If the applicant satisfies the group that he/she is well qualified to be a Christian minister, the Board recommends him/her to the Annual Conference in formal session for admission to that body. The Conference thereupon votes to admit the applicant "on trial." This starts him/her as a *traveling preacher* under appointment by the bishop.

The usual conference novitiate remains on trial for two years. This period gives the conference an opportunity to observe the person's work, since he/she is at once usually put in charge of a pastorate. If the person on trial gives evidence of fitness for and success in the ministry, at the end of a specified time the conference votes to admit him/her into "full connection."

That means being received into full conference membership, which is done in a formal and solemn manner by the bishop who asks such a one, and possibly others who are to be received, certain soul-searching questions in the presence of the entire conference. The questions to be answered were provided by John Wesley himself in order to test and put on record those who were to be admitted to the Methodist preacherhood. They have been asked of every preacher from Wesley's, Albright's, and Otterbein's day to ours and serve to make the candidate declare publicly his or her personal Christian faith and ministerial intent. This having been done and the bishop's examination concluded to the satisfaction of the conference, the bishop puts the name to a vote, and formally receives the candidate— or usually a class or group of candidates—into the conference. This puts him/her into the regular traveling ministry of the entire United Methodist Church. His/her life thereafter until he/she reaches the retirement age set by the General Conference is at the disposal of the Conference with place of service fixed by the bishop.

A traveling preacher may drop out of the traveling ministry and "locate," that is, become a local preacher again if circumstances seem to call for this. Sometimes the illness of a wife or an unusual family situation may forbid a person from continuing in the arduous duties of the pastorate. Sometimes the minister himself recognizes that he/she is not fitted for an itinerant life work and feels that as a local preacher he/she can better serve. In all cases the conference must vote "location" to the person. Sometimes the conference itself locates a person against his/her will if it decides that he/she is a misfit and unacceptable in the traveling ministry.

Ordination

The United Methodist Church confers upon its ministers a special status in providing that under certain carefully outlined procedures each may be ordained to one or both of the two "orders" of the Christian ministry in which United Methodists believe. These are the order of deacons and the order of elders. United Methodist ministers who have been ordained are always recognized by other Christian churches as regular ministers of Jesus Christ.

Deacons

The office of deacon is the lower of Methodism's two orders. It is an ancient one, coming down from the time of the Apostles. Stephen was a deacon, one of the first seven (Acts 6:5), and was a powerful preacher, being full of the Holy Ghost. He was ordained deacon by the Apostles. Philip was another deacon and preacher. "Then Philip went down to the city of Samaria, and preached Christ unto them" (Acts 8:6). Philip expounded the Scriptures to the Ethiopian eunuch and administered to him the rite of baptism.

Deacons were clearly ministers in the early church and are so in United Methodism. A deacon today can (within his/her own charge) perform all the ministerial practices of the church. He/she cannot, however, administer the sacrament of Holy Communion *outside the bounds of his/her own charge,* though such a one can assist an ordained elder whenever requested.

114

Baptists and Presbyterians hold the deacon to be a layperson set apart to look after the temporal affairs of the local church. Most United Methodists, however, agree with Bishop John Emory that the "scriptural evidence for the order of deacons, as an order of ministers distinct from that of elders or bishops, is too plain to be thus lightly treated."

To become a deacon, the Annual Conference must elect a person to "deacons' orders." This having been done, the bishop in a formal rite or ceremony lays his hands upon the head of the person to be ordained and pronounces him/her a deacon in the Church of God. This gives the person permanent ministerial rights. He/she may preach the gospel, bury the dead, marry people where the laws of the state permit, conduct the rite of baptism, and assist in the administration of the sacrament of Holy Communion.

Elders

The highest ministerial order in Methodism is that of elder. The word "elder" is the translation of the Greek *presbyteros* or the Latin *presbyter,* from which came the word "priest" in English. John Wesley did not like the title "priest" (the name the Church of England yet keeps for this order of ministers) and changed it to "elder." United Methodism has kept the name ever since.

A minister who is a deacon may be elected to the order of elders by an Annual Conference. This must also be by formal vote.

The ordination of elders is a much more elaborate ceremony than that of deacons. In this ceremony other elders join with the bishop in placing their hands upon the head of the person to be ordained, while the bishop prays that he/she may be imbued with the Holy Spirit "for the office and work of an elder in the Church of God."

An ordained elder has all the rights and privileges of the Christian ministry in the United Methodist Church. Chief among these is the permanent right to administer the sacraments.

115

Pastors

A Pastor—officially known as a "preacher in charge"—is one who has been appointed to a church or circuit as its regular minister. The chief duties of a pastor are:

1. To preach the gospel, as well as to read and teach the Holy Scriptures.

2. To administer the sacraments, perform marriage ceremonies, and bury the dead.

3. To visit from house to house, so as to give guidance and oversight to church members and to others in need of a pastor's help.

4. To instruct candidates for membership in the church and to receive members and dismiss them upon their request when they move to other locations.

5. To form classes of children and adults in preparation for church membership and to train them for living a Christian life.

6. To have general charge of the worship of the Church in its various ways; to have oversight of other preachers in the pastoral charge; to organize and maintain church schools, United Methodist Women's work, young people's organizations, organizations of United Methodist Men; to see that all the provisions of the *Discipline* are maintained in the pastoral charge and that the ordinances and regulations of the Church are duly observed.

A variety of specific duties are outlined for the pastor in the *Book of Discipline*, and those which we outline above are expressed differently in successive *Disciplines*. However, it is usually admitted that the pastoral office is of most importance to the whole work of the Church. The progress of each local church, both temporally and spiritually, depends on the one who serves it as preacher in charge.

District Superintendents

The District Superintendent is a very important administrative officer in The United Methodist Church. The bishop in charge of an Annual Conference, in making up his appointments, must appoint a certain number of people as district superintendents. To each of these is entrusted the supervision of the churches within a geographic area or district.

In early Methodism such were known as "Presiding Elders," but now they are termed District Superintendents. Their chief duty is to oversee their respective districts continually, and by travel, preaching, and phone to be directly in touch with each charge as a good administrator and so supervise the temporal and spiritual affairs of all their churches. A District Superintendent has charge of the traveling and local pastors in his district; and he may change, receive, or appoint preachers during intervals between conferences in the absence of the bishop. In fact, occasions may arise when a District Superintendent may do everything that a bishop can do except ordain.

The District Superintendent does much of his work through the Charge Conferences, which he must hold in each one of his charges during the year. He is a pastor of pastors; he is a member of the "bishop's cabinet" and thus has a direct part in the making of appointments. He is expected to see that the program of the Church, as outlined by the *Discipline*, is carried out within his district; and he must represent the preachers of his district before the bishop and the other members of the cabinet in all matters having to do with their appointments.

Laymen often fail to realize the significance of the district superintendency in United Methodism. They only see the district superintendent perhaps at one or two of the Charge Conferences during the year and thus do not have full appreciation of the work he does. To a far greater degree than is realized, the whole United Methodist connection functions through the district superintendent. His work, while not always manifest nor spectacular, is felt throughout every department of church and conference work.

Bishops

The bishop in United Methodist polity is the highest officer of the Church and the executive and general administrator of the Church's work and program in the Annual Conferences

117

assigned to him. Bishops are elected by the Jurisdictional Conferences and are *consecrated,* not ordained.

In the Episcopal Church bishops are regarded as belonging to a third order. That church has deacons, elders ("priests," they are called), and bishops. In United Methodism, as has been explained, there are only two orders, deacons and elders; the bishop is simply an elder who is set apart for a peculiar administrative task—that of a superintendent in the Church.

The principal duties of a bishop are:

1. To oversee the spiritual and temporal affairs of the Church.
2. To preside over the General, Jurisdictional, Central, and Annual Conferences.
3. To fix the appointments of the preachers.
4. To form the districts within each Annual Conference.
5. To ordain the elders and deacons after he is authorized to do so.
6. To travel through the connection at large.

Of these duties the most important is that of stationing the preachers. This heavy responsibility is, however, shared by the cabinet of district superintendents, each of whom is largely responsible for the appointments made within his district. But the bishop has the final word, and United Methodism holds him accountable for the way his area is manned and administered.

Administrative Board Members

Up until quite recently the lay officers of each United Methodist Church were largely stewards and trustees, both these groups uniting to form the Official Board. However, while trustees still function under that time-honored title, the 1968 General Conference renamed the Official Board the "Administrative Board," and the title "steward" was supplanted by the specific names of the several officers (work area chairpersons) and members at large who are elected to that Board annually by the Charge Conference.

The *Discipline* provides (as it did in the case of stewards) that those nominated for the Administrative Board shall be "persons of genuine Christian character who love the church, are morally disciplined, are loyal to the ethical standards of the United Methodist Church . . . and are competent to administer its affairs." Youth members are included in the Administrative Board, as well as a number of members at large not specifically assigned any special function. The duties of all these persons are outlined in the *Book of Discipline* in connection with the particular duties they are to perform.

The members of the Administrative Board, as has been noted elsewhere, in effect compose the "cabinet" of the preacher-in-charge, and it is for this reason that the pastor is always made chairperson of the nominating committee in selecting those who are to serve in this capacity. Wise pastors make a point of seeing that the best men and women are selected for membership on the Board and give consideration to the fact that in every local church there are different elements as well as persons of varying talents who should be represented in such a general congregational body.

Each member of the Administrative Board is also a member of the Charge Conference and is expected to attend its meetings, act upon its commissions or committees and fulfill any needed duties. Every church official is of course expected to set an example to the congregation by attendance at church, liberality in giving and by leading a sincere Christian life. "Faithfulness in this office," wrote Dr. H. T. Hudson in speaking of stewards, "is of the highest importance to the welfare of the ministry and the prosperity of the Church."

Laymen and lay women consider it a high honor to be chosen for a place on the Administrative Board. The whole temporal economy of their church rests on the shoulders of these men and women. Generously and unselfishly through the length and breadth of United Methodism they are serving in every local church as coworkers with their pastor and with each other in doing the work of God.

Trustees

Trustees are officials of the local church who have been duly elected to manage the church property. They hold it in trust,

119

not for the local congregation, but for The United Methodist Church.

Each local church must have a Board of Trustees, consisting of not fewer than three nor more than nine persons. Each trustee must be not less than twenty-one years of age, and at least two thirds of them must be members of The United Methodist Church. They are elected by the Charge Conference, each for a term of three years; the elections are so arranged that only one third of each Board of Trustees need be elected in any one year. Trustees are nominated by the Committee on Nominations and Personnel of the Charge Conference. Their election as well as that of certain other church officers, may be delegated to a CHURCH CONFERENCE of the congregation if the Charge Conference decides to have it done that way.

All matters affecting the buying, selling, or mortgaging of church property must be handled through the trustees, though they are expected to carry out the will of the Charge Conference in such important moves. They are looked to to report once a year regarding their work and responsibility. Persons of sound judgment and of substance and repute in the community usually are chosen as trustees. Their duties are not onerous but they are exceedingly responsible, and it is an honor to be depended on as a trustee of The United Methodist Church.

The Itinerancy

A marked feature of United Methodism is the itinerancy of its ministry, that is, the plan of moving ministers from one field of work to another. The itinerant system requires three things:

1. That the congregations give up their right to choose their ministers.

2. That the preachers give up their right to select their own fields of labor.

3. That the appointment be made by a competent, impartial, untrammeled authority (the bishop), whose powers and duties must be outlined carefully and ordered by the whole church.

As the surrender of these rights on the part of the local churches and the preachers is a very real one, it required years of tension, as well as great unselfishness, to establish itinerancy during the formative period of United Methodism. But once having been established, it has justified itself in unmistakable ways.

Our plan of itinerancy is based upon the world-parish conception of Methodism. A preacher in one place must be ready to be a preacher in all places. "Go ye into all the world, and preach the gospel to every creature" has been a command that United Methodism has taken seriously. "Go ye"—not "wait until the people come to you." In a settled, nontraveling ministry the people *call* the preacher; he can accept or reject each call. But in the itinerant system the appointive power tells each preacher what is to be his church and tells each church who is to be its preacher. This is done for an entire Annual Conference of traveling preachers once a year when the appointments are read.

It is not commonly understood even among United Methodists that the appointments *must all be made together* and, therefore, that each depends on the others. Each preacher and each church naturally is interested most of all in his own particular assignment. But every particular appointment is locked in a tight unity with every other appointment, since no preacher can be left without a charge and no charge without a preacher. It is easy enough for a church committee on "pastoral relations" to tell the bishop and district superintendent which man they want or do not want for their preacher. But no one church's wishes can be carried out without affecting the wishes of every other church and minister in the conference. Any undue insistence on the part of a local church, or on that of a minister, to get special wishes carried out in the making of the appointments may break in upon and badly injure the work of other churches or ministers, if such wishes are allowed. This is something which loyal United Methodists should always realize.

Great responsibility rests on the bishop and his cabinet to see that no selfish pressure from any one church, nor from any one minister, no matter how influential, shall keep them from making the very best slate of appointments that can be

121

made. Every good bishop keeps in mind the "care of all the churches," as the apostle Paul expressed it.

The advantages of the itinerant system are:

1. Every preacher gets a place, and every place gets a preacher. Weak churches, as well as strong ones, are always supplied with ministers.

2. There are no leftover preachers and no vacant churches in United Methodism—no unemployed preachers waiting for some church to call them nor any period of waiting between appointments. Local pastors or preachers, as has been explained, are not members of the Annual Conference and make their living in some secular way, preaching when they can. But the regular traveling ministry of United Methodism is composed of men each of whom has a job and is expected to be at work at it.

3. The itinerancy furnishes the people with a variety of ministerial talent and puts each minister on his mettle to lead and serve churches of various types as he continues to travel. The itinerant system is the foe of lethargy, and a succession of different ministers in each church prevents the desuetude that may attend the long pastorate of one man, who may feel tempted to settle down into a ministerial routine.

4. It makes for a wise church strategy and for an efficient manning of all charges, since it gives the appointive power a chance to fill to best advantage every church in the conference. Where a congregation needs a seasoned minister to offset what may have been a former unwise, overenthusiastic, pastoral leadership, or where a young minister may be needed to supply a church which has been too long under an elderly preacher, where a church has burned down and they need a "builder," or a new church has been built and they need a "debt payer," or a preacher is called for to "fill the pews," or a pastor to gather the flock closer together—then the itinerant system gives the bishop and cabinet a chance to pick the very best minister for each special place.

5. It guarantees each minister a pulpit until final retirement. In the churches which call their ministers this is not the case. One may find himself out of a pulpit in middle life, sometimes

through situations over which he/she has no control. And since churches want younger ministers who may be expected to give them a long-term ministry, the displaced minister past middle life may not receive any acceptable calls. To be sure, no ministers in the itinerant system, when they come to waning years will be able to command as large churches as when at the height of their powers—nor should they. But United Methodism finds a place for the minister who must decrease as well as for the young person who is growing in ministerial life.

6. Pastoral changes and adjustments can be more easily made under the itinerant system than under any other. Where a minister does not fit, the embarrassment of requesting a resignation or of voting him/her out, as would be necessary in congregationally governed churches, does not occur. The appointive power in Methodism is simply apprised of the situation, and at the next conference, the person can be moved quietly and another minister put in that place. The violence and strife frequently attending pastoral changes in other connections can thus usually be avoided. Sometimes it is the minister who desires a change, and he/she has the right to suggest to the district superintendent that he/she be moved to another appointment.

7. While both people and preachers give up their rights in the actual making of the appointments, they enjoy the following important safeguards against any arbitrary or ill-considered exercise of the appointive power:

a) Each church has a committee on pastor-parish relations, which must cooperate with the pastor, the District Superintendent, and the bishop in arranging for a change of pastors. This committee is amenable to the Charge Conference and is expected to represent the wishes of the local church. The committee must speak as the Charge Conference directs it to do regarding any move or possible move, any minister or possible minister who may be desired as pastor. The committee on pastor-parish relations is therefore not an independent agency, though a Charge Conference may empower the committee to use its own best judgment in arranging for a change of pastors. This committee of course is advisory only, since the

123

bishop has the final word, but its wishes are heard with great respect by the appointive power.

Since the *Discipline* of the Church provides for an official Committee on Pastor-Parish Relations in every local church, it is expected that the wishes and desires of the local church will be expressed through that committee only. Unofficial requests, private letters to the bishop, and anonymous complaints concerning a pastor are disregarded by the bishop and his cabinet, who very properly look to the official committee on pastor-parish relations to guide them as to what the congregation really wants.

b) Each pastor must be consulted by his district superintendent before a final announcement of his appointment shall be made. Usually any contemplated move affecting a minister is discussed with him/her well in advance of the Annual Conference. This gives the minister an opportunity to express his/her wishes and give an opinion upon the proposed appointment.

c) The bishop must be guided by the members of his cabinet —the district superintendents—in the making of each and all appointments. The case of every minister and every church is represented by the district superintendent in whose district the minister or the church happens to be. No bishop is allowed to make any appointment by private, secret fiat. He must read the entire list of appointments to the entire cabinet before he makes the appointments official by reading them to the Annual Conference.

d) Practically, under the appointive system both people and preachers get their wishes carried out as quickly—sometimes more quickly—than under the "call" system. It is a truism that in the long run every preacher makes his own appointment; each church gets the sort of preacher its challenge and enthusiasm warrant.

Commenting on the itinerant system, a robust Methodist authority of some years ago said, "We believe the plan to be providential; it has worked wonders, and we expect to adhere to it till the trump of judgment sounds." [2]

[2] *Ibid.*

CHAPTER SEVEN

Worship and the Sacraments

United Methodists worship as do other Christians—publicly and privately. The General Rules of our church insist that everyone should "attend upon the public worship of God, the ministry of the Word, the supper of the Lord, and family and private prayer."

Methodist public worship has always been of two types. It is "free" in the usual services of the Church; but it is liturgical, or ordered, in the stated ceremonies called for by our ritual, and in the regular "orders of worship."

United Methodists are free in the sense that we are not bound too closely to any special form or order of worship. We can pray or sing or preach or read scripture at any time, just as may seem fitting to the worshiping congregation or its leader. Early Methodists had a reputation for being completely untrammeled in worship, their spontaneity and enthusiasm being in strong contrast to the stiffness of the Prayer Book and its ordered ceremoniousness. But when we engage in the recurrent rites of the Church, such as Communion, baptism, marriage, funerals, ordinations, and so on, Methodism has always strictly followed a time-honored ritual.

For many years Methodist as well as E.U.B. worship revolved entirely around the sermon. Readings, prayers, and the like were as varied as the congregations that participated in them. After a time the Church began to drop into a regular pattern of worship and at length worked out what we now call our "orders of worship." These are published in the *Hymnal* and in the *Book of Worship*.

125

Many of our people insist that since the Church provides orders of worship, they should be strictly followed in all places without variation. But others say that printed orders are suggestive only, and in the name of Christian liberty feel free to vary them. The introduction to the official *Book of Worship* itself states that this book "is not intended in any way to fetter the spontaneity or reject the reliance upon the Holy Spirit which have characterized Methodism throughout its history. Rather the *Book of Worship* seeks to claim for the Church and its people the total Methodist heritage in worship."

The Orders of Worship

Two Orders of Worship are to be found in the opening pages of the *Hymnal* and in the *Book of Worship*—a "brief form" and a "complete form." Each of these orders outlines a program of hymns, prayers, readings and includes, of course, the sermon. Every congregation is free to modify any chosen order to fit local custom or circumstances.

The Hymnal and Singing

Prominent in every order of worship are the hymns. Methodists and E.U.B. have ever been a singing people. *The Methodist Hymnal,* or *Book of Hymns* as it is sometimes named, is one of the great song books of the world and contains among its 642 hymns a rich wealth of devotional material both in words and in music. It should be known also that the present *Methodist Hymnal* had among its compilers representatives of the Evangelical United Brethren Church who saw to it ahead of time that their cherished hymns were included in what was to be the *Book of Hymns* for United Methodism.

These hymns cover every aspect of Christian life. There are seasonal hymns, such as those for Christmas, Thanksgiving, Easter, and patriotic occasions; there are devotional hymns, penitential hymns, exultant hymns; there are hymns of aspiration and praise; hymns for children, hymns for youth, hymns of social welfare, hymns of the past, and hymns of the present.

Happy the people whose minister is able to develop in them an appreciation of and a love for the hymns made available to them in the *Methodist Hymnal.*

The Reading of the Scriptures

This is a necessary and edifying part of our public worship. Formerly it was done entirely by the minister. Now, however, the participation of the congregation in the public reading of the Word is called for through the use of responsive readings found in the Hymnal. These readings have been carefully chosen, and apply to all the experiences of the Christian life and cover the various seasons of the Christian year.

The reading of the scripture by the minister is done from the pulpit or lectern. Many ministers like to expound as they read, taking a moment or two to explain the context or the special meaning of a particular passage. The Bible, all agree, should always be read reverently and impressively. A substantial lesson, not simply a few verses, most ministers feel, should be chosen on each occasion.

Public Prayer

Public prayer is by its nature at the heart of all Christian worship. There are Christian groups who do not believe in singing, there are those who do not believe in the public reading of the Word, but all religious people believe in prayer. The minister is expected to lead the people in public prayer; and the "pastoral," or "general prayer," called for in our orders of worship, is a special feature which ought never to be neglected. There are ministers who put as much time on the preparation of their public prayers as they do upon the sermon itself. In a true pastoral prayer the minister is praying *for* and *on behalf* of the people, not simply out of some immediate personal feelings of his own.

The *Book of Worship*, compiled by an official Commission on Worship and adopted by the General Conference for optional use among Methodists, contains a well-arranged collection of prayers for both public and private use. This book

127

should be in the homes of our people, for in it can be found a veritable treasury of prayers and acts of devotion.

The Sermon

The sermon has, of course, been the prime feature of United Methodist congregational gatherings since the time of Wesley. We are a preaching church; and while we have been mighty in singing and, we trust, fervent in prayer, yet through the preaching of the Word, United Methodism seems to have borne its greatest witness.

It is not proper, however, to regard the sermon alone as "the service" for everything from the first sound of the organ's voluntary until the final benediction is a part of one unified offering of praise to God.

Other features of Methodist worship, such as the call to worship, offertory, announcements, final prayers, and benediction, likewise have a part in a richly rounded service. The order of worship which each local church adopts for its own, should become familiar to every worshiper so that each person may participate as fully as possible.

Beside the regular orders of worship, provision is made for less formal occasions when Christian people are encouraged to assemble for prayer or praise, for watch night or prayer meeting, for thanksgiving or for comradeship. Evening worship is less formal than that for morning, and evangelistic services are traditionally even more free. Each kind of service has a value in its own way. Reverence and a due regard for the decency and order which should always prevail among Christian people will be the guide, even where printed forms are not provided.

United Methodists go to church as their Christian privilege, being assured that in so doing they will receive a blessing if they bring to the service a proper mind and an open heart. It is not possible to have great preachers in each pulpit. Indeed, with all United Methodism's emphasis on preaching, we have never had in every one of our pulpits men attractive in speech and bearing. But we have had, and now have, sincere, earnest expounders of God's Word, men who have been called and consecrated to the Christian ministry; and these men are endeavoring to give their best from the pulpit Sunday by Sunday. Our people will always find under the ministry of such men spiritual sustenance and help. Every loyal United Methodist should and is privileged to go to church and take his place.

The Ritual

The United Methodist ritual embodies the fixed forms of worship for Communion, baptism, burial, marriage, reception of church members, the ordaining of ministers, and the like. While there is value in varying the program of worship in the usual Sunday service, regularity in conducting the stated rites of the church is demanded by our *Discipline*. "Let our ritual be invariably used," was the old injunction. "A decent ritual," observed Bishop Holland McTyeire, "is the best guard against formality."

John Wesley gave to Methodism the rites and ceremonies which are in our ritual. He took these from the prayer book of the Church of England and revised them slightly. This will explain the likeness of our Communion service, our marriage and burial services, to those of the Episcopal Church, since both the Methodists and Episcopalians took these forms from the same English prayer book. Methodists, however, do not "use the Episcopal Service" any more than the Episcopalians "use" the Methodist service. Both follow what has sometimes been called the "English Rite."

It will not be possible to outline even in the briefest way all the separate offices in the United Methodist ritual. There is one, however—the sacrament of the Lord's Supper—which is so important as the great ordinance and recurrent rite of the Church that the method of its observance should be carefully outlined. Every United Methodist should understand the meaning of the separate readings, prayers, and devotional acts he is summoned to engage in at each celebration of the Lord's Supper.

129

The Order for the Administration of the Sacrament of the Lord's Supper or Holy Communion

The Lord's Supper is perhaps the most sacred service of the Christian Church. Christians everywhere observe it in memory of Christ, who instituted and commanded it. The way the Lord's Supper is observed varies among different groups of Christians, but all celebrate it with the utmost reverence.

United Methodists hold that the Communion of the Lord's Supper is a means of grace and a sign and symbol of the redemptive work of Christ, our Lord. It is both a memorial and a living experience. It is a *memorial* in that through it we remember Christ and the sacrifice he made for us; it is a *living experience* in that each person who reverently engages in it can find it to be an immediate experience of comfort and blessing.

United Methodist churches usually observe communion either monthly or quarterly.

Who may administer the Communion? Regular, ordained ministers of our own or sister evangelical churches are competent to celebrate the Lord's Supper. In United Methodist practice an elder (a minister who has been fully ordained) must always be in charge of a service of Holy Communion. However, if a minister who is not an elder has been appointed to have charge of a special church, he may under certain circumstances as has been before explained conduct the Communion service within the precincts of his own church.

United Methodists may feel free to take the Communion at the hands of any consecrated minister of any other Christian church when they are invited to do so.

Who may communicate? Every member of the United Methodist Church who is in good standing is expected to take Communion when it is made available. The invitation, which is read as a formal part of the ritual, invites those who "truly and earnestly repent of (their) sins, and are in love and charity with (their) neighbors, and intend to lead a new life," to "draw near with faith." Members of other Christian denominations are cordially invited to join with us at the Communion table.

130

Children of the Church who have not yet been admitted to church membership are not usually at the Communion table. There is no fixed rule forbidding them to come, however, and children sometimes come forward with other members of the family. However, as the Communion is considered a privilege of duly admitted church members, children are not encouraged to communicate until they have reached the age of discretion, when they should become members of the Church in their own right and so take their places about the table.

Preparing for Communion

Our church provides two orders for conducting the Lord's Supper. One is a complete formal order, and the other is called "a brief form" for the administration of the sacrament. The complete form is really an order of worship for Sunday morning outlining an entire service of worship with Scripture readings, prayers, offertory, and the sermon all included as a part of this office for the celebration of Communion. This, our present order, varies from the former traditional Communion service which was an entity in itself entirely apart from the sermon and from other "regular" features of Sunday worship.

The main features of the United Methodist sacramental service are set forth below and it is suggested that the reader open to the Communion service as found in the back of the hymnal in order to follow carefully the various features of the service. It is a beautifully balanced rite in which the first prayers and readings are designed to prepare the worshiper for the reception of the Communion itself.

Long custom calls for the Lord's table to have upon it a "fair linen cloth" which covers the "elements," as the bread and wine are termed. The "pure, unfermented juice of the grape" is the symbolic wine called for by our ritual. Methodist and E.U.B. regulations have long been set against the use of fermented wine.

United Methodists come forward and kneel when they receive the Communion, but our church allows persons who have scruples against kneeling to receive the elements either

131

seated or standing. In early days many Protestants felt that kneeling at the Communion table was too suggestive of the Roman Catholic practice of worshiping the Host, as is done in the Mass. But today such scruples are of little weight, and no one who comes to a United Methodist Communion table objects to kneeling.

The Communion service in the first or complete order outlines the entire service and begins with a prelude, hymn, and the congruent features of Sunday morning worship. Then the minister reads certain

Opening Sentences

These sentences are not the traditional offertory sentences which used to be the prelude to the Communion, and which reminded the communicants that they were expected to have ready an offering for the poor. The offering for the poor, however, is still allowed for by a rubric in the main body of the service stating that "where custom prevails an offering may be left by the people at the chancel when they come forward to receive the elements." However, the traditional offertory sentences were changed in 1964 to become Spiritual Sentences introductory to the Communion itself.

After reading one or more of these sentences, the minister says "*the Lord be with Thee* and the people respond with the traditional "*And with Thy Spirit.*" Then after the minister's direction "*Let us pray*" comes the lovely

Collect for Purity

(*Almighty God, unto whom all hearts are open, all desires known. . . ."*)

This is followed by the Lord's Prayer. Here follows

The Gloria in Excelsis

Placing the *Gloria* ("*Glory be to God on high and on earth peace, good will toward men*") at this point in the service, rather than at the last of the Communion office where it was until our last revision, marks a change in the order from that of the Church of England which Wesley followed when he sent us this Rite. After the *Gloria* comes

132

The Invitation

This is the beautiful and traditional *"Ye that do truly and earnestly repent of your sins, and are in love and charity with your neighbors and intend to lead a new life . . . draw near with faith. . ."* Following this the minister and people kneeling, read together the

General Confession

(*"Almighty God, Father of our Lord Jesus Christ, Maker of all things . . ."*) This ancient expression of Christian penitence and plea for mercy has come down from the first Prayer Book of 1549 almost unchanged from the way Archbishop Cranmer wrote it. Read in unison by all, it serves to unite the worshipping congregation in a cry of confession and call for forgiveness.

The Absolution

The Absolution, as it was formerly called, is next. (*"Almighty God, our heavenly Father, who of thy great mercy . . ."*). It is read by the minister and is designed to follow the plea for forgiveness—just made in the General Confession—with the assurance that since God has "promised forgiveness of sins to all them that with hearty repentance and true faith" turn unto him, he will "have mercy upon us; pardon and deliver us from all our sins; confirm and strengthen us in all goodness; and bring us to everlasting life."

The Comfortable Words

These are read next by the minister. (*"If any man sin, we have an advocate with the Father . . ."*) These four sentences are designed to give the worshiper a further assurance of comfort, pardon, and peace.

The General Prayer

Next, since we are following here not merely a Communion service but the whole order of worship for Sunday morning, comes the General Prayer, as it was originally called. This takes the place of the minister's regular pastoral prayer and may be introduced in the service by these words from the pastor: *"Let us pray for the whole state of Christ's Church."*

The text of the prayer is then given. It consists of several petitions which the minister reads and to each of which the people respond with *"Hear us we beseech thee, O Lord."* There are petitions and prayers for the Church universal, for ministers, for people, for those *"who are in trouble, sorrow, need, sickness or any other adversity."* The prayer concludes by making mention of the departed *"who have loved and served thy church on earth and who now rest from their labors (especially those most dear to us whom we name in our hearts before thee").* This petition in the General Prayer was much fought over by the reformers who thought that it was in effect a prayer for the dead. But it does answer a cry of the heart.

(At this point in the longer service we are following, come the Scripture lesson, the Creed, the Sermon, and Notices.)

The Sursum Corda

The mood of the service now suddenly changes. Up to this point there has been a confession of sin and a plea for forgiveness, followed by gentle, comforting words, as the people are prepared more definitely for the reception of Communion. But now the minister suddenly says: *"Lift up your hearts."*

People: *"We lift them up unto the Lord."*

Minister: *"Let us give thanks unto the Lord."*

People: *"It is meet and right so to do."*

The note is of strong, robust thankfulness, and immediately after there follows the exultant *Trisagion.*

Trisagion

"Thrice holy"—the passage from Isaiah. *"Therefore with angels and archangels, and with all the company of heaven, . . . ever more praising thee, and saying: Holy, holy, holy . . ."*

The exultant note now struck brings to the worshiper a feeling of the glory and power of God.

The Prayer of Humble Access

This prayer has traditionally come next. (*"We do not presume to come to this thy table."*) It precedes the Prayer of Consecration in the English prayer book and did so in the M.E. Church, South. It has recently been put after the prayer of consecration. It is a beautiful expression, pleading the right to come to the Communion table not *"trusting in our own righteousness but in thy manifold and great mercies."*

The Prayer of Consecration

(*"Almighty God, our heavenly Father, who of thy tender mercy didst give thine only Son Jesus Christ to suffer death upon the cross for our redemption . . ."*) This prayer is the focus of the precommunion service. Every word of it has been fought over through the ages in an endeavor to make it a true expression of the Christian faith and at the same time to consecrate the elements of the Lord' Supper. It is remembered that the Lord himself blessed the original elements (Matt. 26:26), and Paul speaks of the "cup of blessing which we bless" (I Cor. 10:16). The present prayer does not fix its petition on the *elements*, but on the *communicants*—"that *we* receiving this bread and wine, according to thy Son our Saviour Jesus Christ's holy institution . . . may also be partakers of the divine nature through him."

Following comes the actual communication of the Minister.

Communication of the Minister

The minister, or ministers, take the Communion first, not in order to show any superiority over the people, but better to manage and control the service—"that they may be readye to helpe the chief Minister," the old prayer book used to say.

Receiving the Communion "in both kinds" means both bread and wine. Our church, with all Protestantism, wants to make it explicit that there shall be no denial of the cup to the laity. Both elements are taken at each Communion.

The Communication of the People

By long-continued custom the people come forward and kneel about the chancel rail when the Communion is received.

This is a practice which is to be continued wherever possible. In the interest of time the custom has grown within some churches of passing the elements through the pews where the congregation is seated. But much is lost if the individual worshiper cannot move forward and thus in a public way and by his own act "proclaim Christ's death until his coming again." Each communicant's participation becomes a part of the general witness.

After the people have finished communing, the ministers are directed to place upon the Lord's table what remains of the consecrated elements and cover them with the linen cloth again. Then comes a great prayer in which both minister and people join.

The Prayer of Thanksgiving

It is a matchless petition ("O Lord, our heavenly Father, we, thy humble servants, desire thy fatherly goodness mercifully to accept this our sacrifice of praise and thanksgiving. . . .") Like other parts of this office it is a very old prayer, written by Thomas Cranmer at the time of the Reformation. It ends with a petition that God shall accept our offering of ourselves, "not weighing our merits, but pardoning our offenses; through Jesus Christ our Lord."

The Benediction

The minister pronounces the benediction as the people continue in the attitude of prayer.

Private Communion and Communion in the home are often arranged for the benefit of those who are sick. Here the service is usually much simpler, though the Prayer of Consecration is always to be read. Good ministers know how to adapt this service to the spiritual needs of those to whom they are ministering.

Baptism

Baptism is the other sacrament of the Christian Church. It differs from the Lord's Supper in that while the latter is

136

repeated frequently for people in the full maturity of their Christian lives, baptism is celebrated once and for all in each individual life.

Baptism has always been the gateway to the Christian church. It was so in the early days, and the New Testament gives incident after incident where becoming baptized was equivalent to assuming the pledge of Christian discipleship.

At a very early date children were brought into the church through baptism. Later on it was felt that when children grew to the age of accountability, they should speak for themselves with relation to church membership. So the office of Confirmation was begun in the ancient church and is continued today in the Roman Catholic Church, the Church of England, and the Episcopal Church. The older Methodism for a long time did not adopt the name confirmation for this type of service, calling it the "Form for the Reception of Members." Since 1964, however, it has frankly been termed "The Order for Confirmation and Reception into the Church." It presupposes that those being confirmed have already been baptized.

Infant Baptism

United Methodists together with the great majority of Christians believe strongly in the baptism of infants. Through this act parents dedicate their children to Almighty God, and the church believes that God uses baptism to claim his own and put his seal upon them in a unique way. One authority referred to infant baptism as "matriculation in the school of Christ." "To christen" is the same as "to baptize."

Those who oppose infant baptism do so on the ground that since an unknowing infant can have no awareness of the act of baptism done on his behalf, the rite therefore is meaningless. But overwhelming is the testimony of the Christian ages in which from the earliest days infant baptism has been practiced. Had infant baptism been something which was begun *after* apostolic times, it would have created a revolution in the Church—and of such we do not find the slightest sign. On the contrary we read in the Acts of the Apostles how three

137

thousand were baptized on the day of Pentecost. (Acts 2: 41); and that five households were baptized at other times (Acts 10:48; 16:15, 33; I Cor. 1:16; 16:15). This could scarcely have been possible unless children were included, especially when we remember that Peter preached on the day of Pentecost that the "promise is unto you, and to your children."

Prior to a service of infant baptism the minister is required to talk with the parents concerning the meaning of the baptismal sacrament and the obligation they will be expected to assume, promising to bring up their child in the Christian faith.

Baptism in the home is allowable and is often practiced, but its celebration in the Church is much to be preferred. This gives an opportunity for the congregation, representing the Christian brotherhood, to participate in the service. Also since baptism is the gateway of the Church, it is symbolically fitting that the rite take place in the church sanctuary itself.

United Methodism has never put much stress on the idea of having sponsors, or godparents, at a baptismal service. The Church of England and the Episcopal Church provide for sponsors, the idea being that there should be persons who are not physically kin to the infant who will act as "godkin," or spiritual parents. John Wesley, when he edited the baptismal office for American Methodism, left out the regulation calling for sponsors and made no reference to them.

In United Methodist practice parents are held responsible for presenting their children for baptism and are the ones who are expected to respond. There would be no objection to godparents in a United Methodist baptismal service, and indeed our ritual now refers to "parents or sponsors." But the emphasis with us is upon the great duty of the parents, and *they take the vows for themselves* and not for the child.

The Rite of Baptism

This is carefully outlined in the ritual. The entire office is one that calls for dignity and unhurried celebration of this sacrament of Christ. Those who abridge it in the presence of a waiting congregation so that "time may be saved" may make it a perfunctory and hasty ceremony devoid of that solemnity which should accompany one of the sacred acts of life.

Mode of Baptism

There has been a long controversy in church history over the mode of baptism. In American life this was provoked by Baptists and other aggressive evangelical communions who affirmed that no baptism could be valid unless the body of the believer had been totally immersed in water. United Methodism, with most other Christian bodies, denies this, holding that while immersion is one valid mode, so are sprinkling and pouring equally valid modes.

It is the custom in our church to sprinkle water upon the person being baptized. But if an adult is extremely desirous of being baptized by immersion, our ministers are instructed to let him have his wish.

The appeal to the Scriptures by those who favor immersion in order to determine New Testament practice has always been met with a counter appeal, and no sound New Testament scholar has ever been able to be sure regarding apostolic practice. United Methodists believe that the weight of evidence is in favor of pouring or sprinkling.

Those who support immersion build their argument upon the statement that Christ went to the Jordan to be baptized of John, and so he did. But it is not certain that immersion was the method used. The essential matter in ceremonial washing was that the water should be "living," that is, running water. The Jordan provided living water as did any spring.

Even admitting for the sake of argument that the whole apostolic Church used immersion as its method of baptism (which surely cannot be proved), the living Church of the present would not necessarily feel bound by this mode any more than the fact that the apostles reclined on the floor when they partook of the Last Supper would force us to do likewise today at our Communion services. Symbolism underlies the whole rite, and Christians must be tolerant of one another's practices. If anyone wishes to be immersed, let him be

139

immersed; but let him not deny the validity of the baptism of others who use another mode.

The Baptism of Adults

The service for the baptism of adults is much like that for infants in its general plan of readings, prayers, and so on. The distinctive feature of the adult service, however, is that the person being baptized assumes the vows *by personal response*. No sponsor has ever been thought of in connection with this office.

The vows which are taken during this rite are quite definitive in outlining a person's will and intent. The ancient baptismal vow was a triple one—of "repentance, faith, and obedience." Rather elaborate questions were asked of the convert in former days. Now the minister combines the questions so as to ask for an acceptance of Christ and "an earnest endeavor to keep God's holy will and commandments."

A person must be baptized before he can be formally received into The United Methodist Church. When, therefore, an adult who never has been baptized before is to be received into the Church, it is a common practice on the part of the ministers to combine the service of Adult Baptism with that for the Reception of Members. In such cases the baptism is followed immediately with one further question to the convert. This asks him to certify loyalty to The United Methodist Church, and he pledges that he will uphold it by attendance, prayers, gifts, and service. The minister then welcomes the new member to all the rights and privileges of church membership.

Quite often it is necessary to baptize persons who are ill—perhaps in their homes or at a hospital. Good ministers know how to modify the service for such occasions, and extempore prayer may be a feature. The climax, of course, is the actual administration of baptism to the recumbent individual.

CHAPTER EIGHT

The Church at Work

United Methodism is faith at work. All that has been explained in the previous pages of this book—doctrine, discipline, organization—is intended to come to fruition in the activity and zeal of an energetic Christian people who seek to have God's kingdom come on earth. We are expected to make all our time—even the hours of rest and recreation—count for God. "Never be unemployed; never be triflingly employed," was John Wesley's injunction to his preachers.

In keeping with this spirit Methodism has been a stirring activist movement marked by vigor and energy both in the local congregation and in the general church. Few realize how far-reaching are its manifold activities and how sweeping its ideal. From the smallest congregation to the farthest reaches of the world parish of United Methodism, the energies and personal talents of each individual are expected to find expression in doing the work of God.

There are two ways in which the church's work may be catalogued and described. One is to take it from the standpoint of the general church and classify all activity according to the major functions of church work, as missions, education, publishing interests, evangelism, and so on. Something could profitably be said about these great causes, and a brief description given of the general boards and agencies which look after them. But the other viewpoint, which shall be taken here, is to view the organizational work of the Church from the stand-

141

point of the individual member. What are the activities of his local church? How do these become part of the great structural organization of United Methodism? Most important, how shall one in his local church fit into the grand purpose of God and make his life count in the congregation and community where he lives? These are supremely important questions.

One thing is certain: All the energy and zeal which infuse and sustain the larger work of the church depend on the individual church member. From where he sits in his pew on Sunday morning, though he may not know it, the long, strong lines of United Methodist connectionalism are going out to encircle the world. They go to a United Methodist chaplain ministering to American troops on foreign soil, to a deaconess working in a Wesley House on the Gulf Coast, to a student assisted by the Student Loan and Scholarship Fund of the Division of Education, to an editor of church-school publications planning far ahead for study material, to a lay leader busily supervising his United Methodist Men. To all these and to scores of others, unknown to the ordinary church member, there radiates his influence, his help. If anyone thinks he can go to church to "get away from it all," he will soon find—happily enough both for himself and for the whole connection—that he has really gotten into it all. Even in the peace of Sunday worship one can feel the pulse-beat of the Church universal, a Church that is neither resting nor asleep, but is everywhere a living, breathing organism.

> All one body we
> One in hope and doctrine,
> One in charity.

John Wesley once said that the "Bible knows nothing of solitary religion."

The activities of the Charge Conference and of the Administrative Board have already been described. The various Commissions and "work areas" to be in each church have been outlined in a general way. There are however other local church agencies of great importance. Foremost is the church school.

The Church School

Commonly called the "Sunday school," [1] this is the mightiest of all church agencies. In truth it can scarcely be called an agency at all, since it is the Church itself acting as teacher of its own. The home has a teaching function, and so has the school, and so has the pulpit; but the fact remains that' the Sunday-morning church school provides the only systematic, purposeful instruction in gospel truth and its application to life that Christian people usually receive.

This statement does not discount the duty of parents to inculcate in their children by precept and example the primary and fundamental lessons of Christian living; it is not to forget that every preacher is duty bound to give to both old and young systematic sermonic indoctrination; it is simply to say that the average child of the average United Methodist home must be taught in the church school—if he is systematically taught at all—the deep verities of the Christian faith and of their bearing on life.

Unfortunately even the best of parents scarcely have anything like a regular plan by which they train their children to live Christianly. Usually they try to inculcate the important lessons of life, especially deep moral principles and immediate Christian duties, as each special issue arises. But there is need for a well-integrated study of Bible truth, for the understanding of ethical problems, and for a knowledge of church-wide activities which Christian parents scarcely have time or training to give.

The public school is sometimes depended upon to train children in civic morality and ethical living. It should indeed do its part, but while at best it may be expected to teach lessons of good citizenship and the necessary virtues of honesty and fair dealing, it is handicapped even in this regard by the decision of the courts that no religion at all may be taught within its confines. This cuts the nerve of anything positive the school

---

[1] Church school is the proper name for the inclusive teaching functions of all departments of each local church. Sunday school is that part of it which meets Sunday morning.

143

may do, for *without religion all ethical systems sooner or later collapse.* Only the Church, basing her teaching on the everlasting gospel, can establish a proper regard for man because it teaches first one's primary obligation to God. *Unless children are taught Christian truth in the church school, they will rarely be taught it regularly and systematically anywhere.*

United Methodism to date has not failed to recognize this truth. Its Sunday schools were a part of its program from the earliest days. Susanna Wesley gave religious instruction in the Epworth rectory—including her own numerous brood—long before Robert Raikes began his first formal Sunday school. John Wesley saw to it that his Savannah parish had a Sunday school with regular classes.

As later on the Methodist and Evangelical and United Brethren churches grew, their church schools kept pace with their growth. The measure of any church's life and vigor can best be found not in the number of adult members on its rolls nor in the salary paid the minister but in the number enrolled in the church school. "No matter how important a church appears to be," one of our bishops said, "if it has not got a good Sunday school, that church is on the way to the cemetery." He added, "It may take a long time to get there—but get there it will."

To promote and supervise United Methodist schools, the General Conference has established a Section of Local Church Education in its larger Board of Discipleship. The Church also provides for the publication of a complete body of church school literature. This is systematized and graded to fit the various ages and is arranged to cover all subjects on which Christian people should be taught.

In providing literature, The United Methodist Church cooperates with other Christian denominations in producing the International Sunday School Lessons. So general is the use of these coordinated lessons in Protestantism that a Methodist authority once called the church school "the greatest theological seminary in Christendom." The Church also produces many other types of lesson material.

A successful church school depends on:

144

1. The self-sacrifice and ability of officers and teachers in each church school. Such persons must give freely their own time and attention to the work, and at considerable cost to themselves. Their Sunday, their day of rest, must be drawn upon for the sake of others. But let this be said to our church school teachers: The rewards are greater than the cost. A faithful church school teacher fulfills a mission scarcely inferior to that of the ministry itself. Many stalwart Christians today can testify to the abiding influence of some well-remembered church school teacher during their formative years.

2. The interest and support of the pastor and Administrative Board of the Church. Nominal interest and benevolent well-wishing are not enough. The pastor must give his time, the officials of their means, to provide the proper facilities. It is a sad commentary on any church when in connection with an imposing sanctuary the church school rooms are comparatively bare and poorly appointed.

3. The general attendance of the people—old as well as young. There are classes for every age and study materials to suit all manner of needs. Parents should take their children—not send them.

The church school is not only the training ground but the recruiting agency of the Church. Out of its classes come the boys and girls who are to become church members when they reach the age of discretion. In its leadership are to be found the most substantial "pillars"—to use St. Paul's word—of any congregation. The Church of the future is largely the church school of the present.

United Methodist Women

In every local church there is, or should be, an organized unit of United Methodist Women. This is the name given in 1972 to the combination of the Women's Society of Christian Service and Wesleyan Service Guild. All the organizational work of the women members of The United Methodist Church is carried on through this huge organization. It has sometimes been called the "largest women's club in the world," for in the breadth

145

of its activities, the sweeping nature of its program, the amount of Christian work it accomplishes, and the tremendous enrollment it possesses, there is nothing comparable to United Methodist Women. Perhaps in no other organization have women banded themselves together so efficiently as they do in the volunteer work of this vast church group.

Organically United Methodist Women comprise a division of the Board of Global Ministries. However, since it has its own officers, its own budget, it functions as a reasonably autonomous organization. It owns schools, colleges, hospitals, homes, social centers, orphanages, rescue homes, and mission stations in many "faraway places with strange-sounding names." It supports missionaries and deaconesses who are commissioned under the authority of the general Church.

In each local church this organization provides for women their most natural channel for religious activity. It is not, however, true to say that the United Women afford the *only* sphere of activity for United Methodist women. Women serve as stewards, trustees, Sunday school superintendents and teachers, and frequently represent the Church in Annual and General Conferences, and on the committees and commissions of the general church. It is a fact, however, that United Methodist Women in its varied program and comprehensive interests, provides each woman of the Church with an opportunity to use her personal talents to best advantage.

The *Discipline* says: "The organized unit of United Methodist Women shall be a community of women whose purpose is to know God and to experience freedom as whole persons through Jesus Christ; to develop a creative, supportive fellowship; and to expand concepts of mission through participation in the global ministries of the church." (1972 *Discipline*, ¶ 160.3, 1156 *Article* 3).

In keeping with this announced aim the unit in the local church divides its work and responsibilities into various departments. These vary from time to time but usually take in missionary education, Christian social involvement, local church activities, spiritual growth, program resources, and the like. Each local unit elects its president, its vice president, recording secretary, and treasurer. Meetings are held regularly, and the general educational and promotional program of the organization is systematically put into effect. The mission-study classes of United Methodist Women, with their regular and comprehensive coverage of mission interests and concerns, have been of untold value in deepening and broadening the mind of the whole Church.

United Methodist Women through the systematic giving of its members and the careful management and expenditure of its funds is able to carry on a colossal program. The amount contributed for overseas and home mission work in any one year runs into several millions, and twice as much is contributed by the women to their own local churches. The average administrative board member, when told what the United Methodist Women in his own church has given to all causes in any one year, is apt to express both amazement and admiration.

It is the goal of this organization to enlist every woman of the Church in its ranks. It has been growing in numbers each year and at last reporting there were well over a million and a half members while its budget approximates fourteen million dollars for all areas of work.

Lay Activities

The United Methodist Church is a layperson's church. While ministers in the last reported statistics numbered almost thirty-five thousand, the lay membership of the Church registered ten and a half million. Lay persons have equal representation with ministers in the great General and Jurisdictional Conferences, and thus share equal responsibility in making laws, electing church executives, and shaping general policies. The 1972 General Conferences proposed a plan* for equalizing the ministerial and lay representation in the annual conferences. For while there are lay representatives from every church in the Conference, there are more ministers than churches due to the fact that many ministers are chaplains, teachers, editors, and the like, while retired ministers, of course, continue to be voting members in their own annual conference.

* This plan is now in effect.

As is well known, in the Administrative Board in each local church, lay persons comprise the great majority and do their full part in looking after the affairs of their own local church.

Both The Methodist Church and the Evangelical United Brethren Church had powerful lay organizations at the time of their union. These came together at union as United Methodist Men and function strongly in The United Methodist church. The overhead work of the laity in the Church heads up in the Division of Lay Life and Work in the Board of Discipleship of the Church.

"Lay activities," Bishop Costen J. Harrell properly stated, "is a program rather than a society." And what a program! "The Division of Lay Life and Work shall have the responsibility to interpret and spread through the Church all the rich meanings of the universal priesthood of believers, of Christian avocation, and of the ministry of the laity. It shall help the Annual Conferences and the local churches in programs which aim to recruit and to equip the laity—children, youth, men and women—for the widest and most productive ministry possible through the Church." (Discipline, 1972, ¶ 1024)

In pursuance of this mandate the *Discipline* outlines many important functions all of which direct the Board how it should carry on its important work. These include Christian fellowship, personal evangelism, lay speaking or preaching, circulation of church papers and Christian literature, support of the ministry, overseeing the finances of the Church, attendance upon worship services and participating in the district and conference lay organizations when called upon to do so. All manner of Christian activities are expected of persons chosen to participate in the general lay activities of the Church.

It is sometimes assumed that if a man is not a member of the Administrative Board, he will not find the opportunity to do systematic constructive work for his church. This is not true. To utilize the vast manpower of United Methodism, the General Conference has created a men's organization known as the United Methodist Men and at the same time outlined for it a broad program of lay activities building into those which we have mentioned above.

A special responsibility of the United Methodist Men is to promote stewardship, personal evangelism, and lay speaking. Especially committed to its care is the stewardship-of-possession program; this emphasizes the need and worth of systematic Christian giving.

The chairman of United Methodist Men is a member of the Administrative Board by virtue of his office.

In both the Evangelical United Brethren and Methodist churches there were lay leaders called for and elected in every charge, these having great responsibility, as their names indicate, in guiding the activities of the laymen and women in every church. There are also conference lay leaders who are now members of their own Annual Conference at its sessions and expected to head up many general moves among the people of the Conference. This office has proved helpful in many ways that make for progress in The United Methodist Church.

Every church must today have a lay leader, who is elected yearly by the Charge Conference. The lay leader has no organization as such over which he presides, but he is an independent officer of the church. He is thus able to promote, in cooperation with the pastor and board chairperson, the entire program of lay activities.

The lay leader may be elected chairperson of the Administrative Board, or as is often the case, the chairperson of the board is automatically made lay leader. He/she is given a sweeping mandate to lead the local congregation in all sorts of helpful church work. In instances where more than one church is on a charge, each one of those churches must elect its own lay leader.

The district lay leader is elected by the Annual Conference on nomination of the district Committee on Lay Life and Work each year. The Annual Conference lay leader is elected by the conference on nomination of the Conference Committee on Lay Life and Work. In each jurisdiction there is a jurisdictional secretary of lay activities, and in the general church there is an executive secretary of the Board of Discipleship and the Division of Lay Life and Work for the whole connection.

Interest in lay persons' work apart from Administrative Board

149

duties has grown in The United Methodist Church during recent years. It may be expected to increase even more as the church continues to enlarge its program.

United Methodist Finances and General Funds

"The work of the Church requires the support of our people, and participation therein through service and gifts is a Christian duty and a means of grace." So the book of *Discipline* introduces its important directions regarding the financial system of The United Methodist Church. In that system there are:

GENERAL FUNDS—Determined by the General Conference and raised by the whole Church to carry on its connectional work (missions, education, and so on).

ANNUAL CONFERENCE FUNDS—Determined by each Annual Conference and used to carry on special Annual Conference causes (orphanage, conference paper, and so on).

LOCAL CHURCH FUNDS—Determined by the Administrative Board and/or the Charge Conference to carry on the work of the local church (minister's salary, janitor, fuel, church repair, and so on).

In addition there may be *jurisdictional funds*, if a Jurisdictional Conference decides to ask its component Annual Conferences and charges to support some special jurisdictional project (as a headquarter's office or executive secretary). Or there may be *district funds*, from which district stewards may make apportionments for the district superintendent or for a district parsonage or for carrying on district missionary work.

Since all funds and budgets are eventually to be raised by the members of the local churches, it is the practice of many churches to incorporate in the local-church budget the total amount that the church is expected to give to all causes. Thus the dollar in the collection plate is subject to division and subdivision until a proportionate part of it has been put into every approved activity of the general and local church.

The General Funds

The big general funds and budgets of The United Methodist Church must each be prepared and recommended to the

General Conference by the Council on Finance and Administration. When adopted by the General Conference, they become the general budget of the church for the ensuing four years.

The General Conference also decides the basis on which each fund is to be apportioned to the Annual Conferences or to the local church. Most funds are based upon a fixed budget—that is, one which has been estimated and adopted in advance as an overall amount to be raised during the year or perhaps during the next four years. Most of the general boards of the church, however, receive a set percentage of the World Service dollar as World Service funds come in. These percentages are fixed by each General Conference for the ensuing four years and must be strictly adhered to. They can be deviated from only in direst emergency.

Succeeding General Conferences revise the general church budget and vary the respective percentages each board or agency receives as need may demand. New causes and new funds may of course be provided for by future General Conferences as new situations arise.

At present the established general funds are:

The World Service Fund—This gigantic fund supports all the World Service agencies of the church. These agencies are such organizations as the Board of Global Ministries, Board of Discipleship, theological schools, Board of Pensions, and so on.

The General Administration Fund—This provides for the expenses of the General Conference sessions, the Judicial Council, the statistical office, and such commissions and committees as may be constituted by the General Conference. This enables them to do their work through the four years until the next General Conference meets.

The Episcopal Fund—This fund supports the bishops, retired bishops, widows of bishops, and minor children of deceased bishops. It has been obtained by the General Conference asking from each Annual Conference an amount equal to a fixed percentage—this has been something like 2 percent of the total of the salaries paid the ministers of that conference. The Annual Conference may apportion out this amount to the local churches on any basis they please, but usually they follow

151

the percentage-against-the-minister's-salary plan just as the General Conference has handed it down to them.

The Interdenominational Cooperation Fund—This fund is the Church's contribution to the work of the National Council of Churches, the World Council of Churches, the World Methodist Council, and to support moves made in the interest of ecumenical church cooperation.

The Ministerial Education Fund is one which has become increasingly important of late years as the seminaries of the United Methodist Church and the ministers being trained in them need to be generously and effectively supported.

There are from time to time established special funds such as what is at present known as the *Temporary General Aid Fund*. The purpose of this fund is to raise the level of the pensions and minimum salaries of the former Central Jurisdiction Conferences and the Rio Grande Conference and their successors. The apportionment and distribution of this fund is made the responsibility of the Council on Finance and Administration.

Annual Conference Funds

As has been explained, each Annual Conference has the right to establish its own budget for its own benevolences and causes. This budget is drawn up and presented by the Conference's Council on Finance and Administration after that Council has inquired into all the causes which the Conference may be asked or expected to support. When approved and adopted this becomes what is commonly called the Annual Conference Benevolence Budget. It is used chiefly for projects within the Conference, and there is no overlapping between the items of this budget and that of the general funds.

However in assigning to each local church its share of the general and Conference Benevolence Budget, it is mandatory to put these two funds together and apportion out the combined amount as the World Service and Conference Benevolence Budget. Here is how this is done: Each local church is notified at the beginning of each conference year what amount has been apportioned to it for its share of the combined budget.

The *Discipline* suggests that the pastor and lay leader shall there-upon "present" to the Church—and to every church on a circuit—the amount asked with an explanation of each cause to be supported. So ample opportunity is given for a discussion of the local church apportionment *before* it is officially put before the Charge Conference. The members of that conference are therefore ready, when the apportionments are presented, to accept, to increase or to request a less amount which their charge is asked to assume.

In practice, since the element of compulsion is not present and since the apportionments are made by conference and district representatives who know what is equitable, charges usually take pride in assuming the amount expected of them. Often they assume more than they are asked, and even more often, churches overpay at the year's end their apportionments.

United Methodists are encouraged to give to special causes or special projects when these are approved by the General Church or by the Conference Council on Finance and Administration. An amount paid to a "special"—say for a mission building in Finland or the salary of a medical missionary in Bolivia —can be credited to the local church's share of general funds if properly authorized and sent through proper channels. Special appeals for causes not listed in the regular budgets of the church are looked upon with disfavor, except in cases of emergency. Indeed the *Discipline* directs that no appeal can be made to a local church unless the cause represented has been properly approved by the Conference Council on Finance. Since all worthy causes are expected to be reviewed by that Council when formulating the budget, it is assumed that causes which have been approved are in every way worthy and that causes which have not been approved should not be allowed to make special appeals to local churches. This blocks out sporadic pleas and casual collections taken publicly in church and enables our church people to underwrite and support in a stronger way those Christian moves and projects of most value.

It is evident from the above that when a United Methodist puts his or her dollar in the collection plate as part of one's pledge for the year, it is divided in many parts. Usually the greater part of it goes to the local church. Of the remainder, the District and the Annual Conference, and always the big funds of the General Church get a certain share. "We give," a former *Discipline* said truly, "that all members of The United Methodist Church may share in its manifold ministries at home and abroad, and that the work committed to us may prosper."

General Church Agencies

The general agencies of the Church which are known as World Service Agencies are those which are supported by the World Service Fund. The United Methodist Publishing House is not a World Service Agency as it supports itself, and indeed gives its profits to the support of the retired ministers and other conference claimants. But the great causes of missions, education, evangelism, lay activities, health and welfare, pensions, the American Bible Society and other important interests of the Church are taken care of by appropriate boards and organizations created by the General Conference.

It is not within the scope of this work to give a detailed study of the structure and work of the various boards entrusted with the oversight of the manifold work of The United Methodist Church. All such have recently been sweepingly recast by the General Conference and further changes in structure and responsibilities may be expected from time to time for the better fulfilling of their work. The current *Discipline* must be referred to for all such organizational patterns. Suffice it to say that all the important interests of our great Church are carefully cared for and directed, that United Methodism under God may fulfill its comprehensive mission as a world Christian church.

CHAPTER NINE

United Methodists and Other Churches

Methodists enjoy cooperating with other Christian churches. We have been foremost in moves looking toward Christian unity. The Ecumenical movement—the trend toward union of all churches—is being supported in every way by United Methodists. While we hold tenaciously to our beliefs, we grant all other Christians the right to hold to theirs provided that they show by deed and profession that they are sincere followers of Jesus Christ. We, therefore, respect one another's Christian fellowship, covet one another's good will, appreciate the opportunity to join in others' worship and have them join us in ours.

We put up no bars preventing members of another church from partaking of the sacrament with us, but are glad to have them do so. We extend the right hand of fellowship to all sincere seekers, but we do not proselytize those who belong to another Christian communion. When members of other Christian churches profess a desire to join ours we receive such persons without requiring them to renew any of the Christian vows they had taken when first they joined their church. When one of our own members wishes to unite with another church, we give him a letter commending him to the love and care of the church which he wishes to join. "Break not the brotherhood" is a United Methodist principle.

The United Methodist Church has an official agency known as the Division on Ecumenical and Interreligious Concerns which has power to treat with all other church bodies with regard to cooperative moves or specific plans for organic union. It can initiate on its own responsibility such moves, and continues to meet with like representative bodies of other churches. United Methodists have always had the reputation of being great "joiners."

United Methodism contributes financially to such common causes as the American Bible Society, the World Council of Churches, and the National Council of Churches. The first president of the Federal Council of Churches, organized in 1908, was a Methodist Bishop, Eugene R. Hendrix. Since that time Methodist and Evangelical and United Brethren officials and representatives have been leaders in all the work of the Federal Council, the World Council and now the National Council of Churches. Bishop Reuben H. Mueller of the Evangelical United Brethren Church was president of the National Council of Churches at about the time of the Methodist-E.U.B. union.

Since our people live among and wish to cultivate and continue friendly relations with all religious groups, it will be helpful to set forth our attitude toward the doctrines and practices of other large churches. It is obviously impossible to treat here all the churches and sects met with in American life, but the following five churches are taken because of their numbers and influence and their close economic and social ties with our people.

United Methodists and Roman Catholics

We believe the Roman Catholic Church to be a true Church of Jesus Christ, but that it is weighted down and covered over with practices and doctrines representing more the traditions of men than the truths of God. We respect and admire that church for some of its tenets and practices, but we differ with it profoundly in others.

We are one with the Roman Catholics in allegiance to God as Father, to Christ as Lord and Savior, and to the Holy Spirit as guide and counselor. We affirm belief in a Holy Catholic Church, but that Church is to us broad and universal, never narrow and exclusive. We join with the Roman Catholics in reverencing saintly men and women of the past who set an example to all of us. We appreciate the unremitting missionary efforts of Roman Catholicism and its vast works of charity carried on in hospitals, orphanages, rescue homes, and the like. We admire the peculiar type of personal piety which Rome often cultivates among its people and the deep saintliness frequently manifest. Above all we appreciate the way the Roman Catholic Church holds up the cross of Christ and exalts the sacrifice of our Lord at all times and in all places.

With all Protestantism we have rejoiced during these last few years at the more brotherly way in which the Roman Catholic Church has begun to deal with Protestants whom Pope John XXIII called, in an epochal statement, "separated brethren." The word *brethren* was for Roman Catholics a great concession, and since then the overtures and moves made by both groups across the deep gulf formerly fixed between them are very encouraging.

But with all that we continue to differ with Roman Catholics:

1. In their dependence on an earthly church and the pope of Rome as the final authority in matters of religion. We deny the doctrine that the pope is infallible when he speaks *ex cathedra,* (that is formally and officially) since he is after all only a man. We deplore the dominance of the priesthood in the Roman Church and its teaching that the priest has power to grant absolution for sins. We hold that every Christian man or woman is his or her own priest and that all believers constitute a priesthood whose influence and leadership help each and all to live closer to God.

2. We deny the Roman Catholic teaching that Christ's body is made to appear in the Mass at the word of the priest. We consider it a travesty to worship relics or bless medals or use "holy water." We deplore the idea that man can be saved by *what he does,* and it appears to many that the entire Roman Catholic system becomes in effect a salvation-by-works process.

3. We deny that one can be truly pardoned from sin by doing penance or may gain merit by performing pilgrimages

157

or lighting candles or making vows; we deny that there is a purgatory and consider it a delusion to say masses for the dead.

4. We have always objected fiercely to the assumption by Rome that it alone is the Church, and that only its bishops and priests are true ministers of God. We deny that Rome can even claim to be catholic, for catholicity is *inclusive* and not *exclusive* as the Roman Church has traditionally made it.

5. We object to the Roman Catholic practice of forbidding people to hear opposing points of view or to read books which they consider to set forth hostile doctrine. We hold to the American—and Protestant—principles of the open Bible, the open forum, the unfettered press, and the unhindered spread of ideas. We believe that truth is its own best witness and that Christian people should be allowed to sift for themselves all ideas affecting their own welfare. History makes clear that the countries which have long been under Roman Catholic domination have failed to grow intellectually, morally, and even physically as have the Protestant nations.

6. We discourage marriage between Protestants and Roman Catholics, feeling that such marriages, while sometimes successful, are always threatened with heartache and family dissension. The Roman Catholic party to a mixed marriage is under the dominance of the priest and either must obey his instructions with regard to bringing up children and in all the intimate matters of the home, or must refuse to obey them. In either case there is unhappiness and tension. "Don't marry a Roman Catholic" is a sound injunction for United Methodist youth to keep in mind.

It is clear, therefore, that we are in disagreement with many Roman Catholic beliefs, but that by no means implies a personal hostility toward Roman Catholics as individuals. They are our friends and neighbors, and we shall trust them as such. We are at variance with their *system*, not with *them*.

United Methodists and Episcopalians

Methodists are closely akin to Episcopalians doctrinally and liturgically, as both churches originated in the Church of

England and inherited the same rites and the same Articles of
Religion. That there are great psychological differences between the two is undeniable, but these great churches have
learned more and more to appreciate each other.

United Methodists admire the Episcopal Church:

1. For its emphasis on the Church as the Body of Christ.
Representing an entity which transcends and holds together all
local churches in one august body is the Church—Holy, Catholic, and Universal—not a congeries of separate, local congregations, but a transcendent unity, the Bride of Christ.

2. For its *Book of Common Prayer* and a stately ritual in
which words and ideas are fittingly blended in a majestic offering of praise and worship.

3. For the way in which by systematic and well-chosen readings and lessons from the Holy Bible the people are guided
through the church year. Each season has its own special message, each emphasizes some part of the work of Christ for his
Church.

4. For the wise use of symbols in building and altar, the
reverence for the house of God, giving to God, through worship, of our very best—in all these things we deeply appreciate
the contribution of the Episcopal Church to the Church
universal.

We disagree with the Episcopal Church over:

1. The doctrine of apostolic succession. This doctrine holds
that from the days of the apostles on there has been a chain
of ordinations with one generation of bishops ordaining another and these in turn ordaining priests, so that the Church's
orders go back in uninterrupted succession to the time of the
apostles. This theory, John Wesley once said, "No one ever
has proved, nor can prove."

2. We disagree with the belief that no one can administer
the sacrament nor can be truly ordained except by one who
is in the apostolic succession. We affirm that God only knows
whom he has truly ordained and that the "test of apostolic succession is apostolic success."

3. We do not favor too much rigidity in worship even when
a stately prayer book furnishes the norm. We adopt robes and

vestments and a clerical dress for certain functional purposes, but United Methodists are still afraid of "formality."

4. We do not follow the Episcopal idea that the office of bishop is a "third Order," thus making the bishop an ecclesiastical superior to his brethren. In United Methodism the bishop is an elder set apart to be an administrator, having no unique spiritual power save the right to ordain—and his power to ordain must be granted in each instance by Annual Conference vote. This power is something given by the Church to the bishop, not by the bishop to the Church.

5. We do not believe that in order to join the Church, one must be confirmed by the laying on of hands of a bishop, though we respect Confirmation. We receive persons into the Church through our pastors, and while our Reception of Members is a close replica of the Office of Confirmation in the Episcopal Church, there are profound differences between the underlying philosophies manifest in these separate rites.

Nevertheless United Methodists and Episcopalians feel a close kinship which the years have served to deepen. Each has influenced the other to the advantage of both.

United Methodists and Baptists

United Methodists and Baptists are at one in their common evangelical heritage and purpose; in their deep conviction regarding the fatherhood of God, the lordship of Christ, the presence of the Holy Spirit, the Bible as the Word of life, and the need to live lives which show forth the glory and promise of the gospel.

We appreciate the Baptists:

1. For their emphasis on the sacrament of baptism—though not upon the insistence in some of their churches upon immersion as the only mode. It can be truly said that as their name implies, the Baptists have built their church largely about a Sacrament of Christ.

2. For their intense loyalty to their own fellowship. Baptists have no "connection," as we United Methodists would term it. "There is no Baptist Church," said one of their

authorities. "There are only Baptist churches." Yet these churches stick together in a tight comradeship which can teach much to other denominations more highly centralized in their form of organization.

3. For their aggressive gospel proclamation, evangelistic zeal, and making religion real in national life. Where other fellowships may falter and fail in political or economic moves for civic and national righteousness, you can count on the Baptists. United Methodists and Baptists traditionally have stood shoulder to shoulder in all battles for public morality.

We differ with the Baptists:

1. In the insistence in most of their churches upon immersion as the only valid mode of baptism. We do not sympathize with the practice which certain Baptist churches (though not all) follow of "close communion"—that is, of admitting only baptized (immersed) Christians to their Communion table; and we deplore the exclusiveness which inevitably appears among those who insist that a particular rite (baptism by immersion) is the only true gateway to the Church. Any insistence on the mechanics of a rite denatures the spirit of it.

2. We do not agree with their once greatly stressed teaching —or that of certain of their theologians—that when once a person has been saved from sin, he will ever after remain saved to the end. We wish that this might prove true, but experience and life teach otherwise. In the Baptist view a believer who later falls has never been saved at all. Obviously there is no way to tell whether he has or has not, but to a Methodist this theory does not comport with reason or with life.

3. We differ, or have differed, with the Baptists when they call in question the United Methodist teaching that we are expected to live sinless lives. Certain Baptist leaders and theologians have held that the commandments of God are given as guides and ideals, but that it is not expected that these commandments can be kept. Against this challenge to the doctrine of perfection our Methodist fathers heatedly responded by saying that God would not have given us commands he did not expect us to obey.

In spite of these differences United Methodists and Baptists socially and economically are much the same sort of people. They have worked together well and will continue to work together in all moves for social and national betterment and for bringing on earth the kingdom of God.

United Methodists and Presbyterians

With Presbyterians we traditionally have differed in doctrine, but worked well together in practice. The doctrinal differences have lain chiefly in the heavy Calvinistic emphasis insisted on by Presbyterians of an earlier day. Then an ironclad predestination was opposed to Methodism's affirmation of universal atonement. As the years have gone by and the Calvinistic emphasis has been softened, United Methodist and Presbyterian congregations have drawn much closer together. In patterns of worship, in social, political, and economic issues, we are perhaps closer to the Presbyterians than to any other large body of Christians.

United Methodists appreciate:

1. The Presbyterians' emphasis on the sovereignty of God, so long as that sovereignty is not thought of as destroying the freedom of man's will. Over against the weak teaching of certain modern liberals that God is unable to break through his own natural laws, or that he is the embodiment of a supine benevolence, the Presbyterians rightly see God high and lifted up, the sovereign Ruler and majestic Creator of the universe. The Church universal needs to have that truth stressed.

2. The solid racial stock behind the Presbyterians—Dutch, Swiss, and especially Scottish—the sturdy way their ancestors fought both against the papal power and in Scotland against the Church of England when their Christian liberty was imperiled. There has always been considerable iron in the Presbyterian blood, and Christianity is richer for it.

3. Their emphasis on learning and on an educated ministry. They have put into practice John Wesley's celebrated exhortation "Let us unite the two so long divided—knowledge and vital piety." Presbyterians have always demanded that their

ministers be well-trained men, and the universities in Scotland and the famous institutions they have built in our own land witness to the intensity of their search for truth. We can thank their scholars for leadership in many fields of Christian interest.

United Methodists disagree with the Presbyterians whenever they so emphasize the sovereignty of God as to permit logic to supplant fact in viewing Christian experience. Also we do not like a certain rigidity that is sometimes found in Presbyterian thought, nor the regimentation of their theological and ministerial mind under the stamp of a fixed educative process. These features, however, are not as obtrusive today as formerly, and our people live more and more in Christian unity with the Presbyterians.

United Methodists and Lutherans

The Lutheran Church is largely composed of those whose forebears came from Germany or the Scandinavian countries. Lutheran congregations have never become as widely distributed over the United States as have some of the other Protestant denominations. Nevertheless Lutherans are unusually strong in certain localities, especially where immigration brought large numbers from Germany or Northern Europe.

United Methodists and Lutherans agree on all the important verities of Christianity as these are stated in the Apostles' Creed. Especially do we appreciate the Lutherans for the seriousness of their pastoral leadership. It means something to a Lutheran home for the pastor to make a call, and there is nothing perfunctory about his visit. He may examine the children as to their Christian attitudes, or he may enjoin the parents as to some special duty they should perform. He takes seriously his duty as pastor, and so do the people.

Lutherans guard well the table of the Lord, and while they admit others than Lutherans to their sacramental services, they let it be known that this is no light privilege.

Lutherans because of their training and their racial heritage do not easily become members of other Protestant Churches.

Their indoctrination and organization tend to build them into a more self-centered communion than characterizes the usual American church. Nevertheless they are a solid Christian people whose personal piety, training, and character we may well emulate.

United Methodists and Smaller Church Bodies

Enough has already been written concerning United Methodist doctrine and polity to make clear what attitude United Methodists may be expected to take toward church bodies not treated in the pages above. In matters of polity (internal church organization) we all agree that each church has a right to decide for itself what form of government it shall have. There is therefore no quarrel with any body of Christians who may prefer a congregational polity (in which the congregation by democratic rule manages everything) or presbyterial (in which a group of elders directs matters) or episcopal (with bishops as chief officers). Curiously enough, United Methodist polity is a combination of these three organizational forms. We would never claim, however, that our polity is better than that of others. We simply say that it suits us best, and we will respect the claim of any other Christian group which says the same for its organizational pattern.

United Methodists have frequent contact with certain of the so-called enthusiastic sects and with minor groups which emphasize what they believe to be New Testament manifestations of spiritual phenomena appearing among them. Some of these bodies stemmed out of the Methodist movement in years past. It behooves us to deal gently with them. We appreciate the zeal, the intensity, and the announced quest for holiness among those groups which make this last their aim and ideal. We deprecate a certain narrowness and exclusiveness shown by many of these smaller bodies and feel that their crass literalism precludes them from taking advantage of the broadness and sweep of a true catholic, or universal, Christianity. They do much good work, however, and shame us by going into situations and among people whom Methodism does not seem to reach as it once did.

The United Methodist Church and World-Wide Methodism

United Methodism has spread over the world and is at home in almost every land. Separate Methodist churches have of course been organized. Some of these are very large bodies. While holding to the same doctrine and rules of personal discipline, these churches differ from one another markedly in forms of organization. British Methodism, for instance, has no bishops; and neither had the Canadian Methodists before they went into the Church of Canada.

The Methodist churches of the world send representatives periodically to a World Methodist Conference, which meets once every five years. This conference, while having no power to pass any laws that may be binding upon its constituent members, gives an opportunity for fellowship and fraternity, and for considering all that affects present-day Methodism everywhere. Its endeavor is to deepen mutual understanding and to encourage and inspire the world-wide brotherhood of the followers of Wesley.

The World Methodist Conference elects a World Methodist Council, which is empowered to prepare and plan for succeeding World Methodist Conferences. The council also acts as an advisory group dealing with all questions that may arise among Methodist bodies in different nations. Within recent years world Methodism has become much better integrated than ever before through its world conferences and its World Methodist Council. Wesley's dream of a world parish is becoming a reality to the Methodists who continue to carry on his work—and God's—in our day.

Goals for a Christian's Striving

To *know* God and settle my soul's salvation once and for all with a deep, quiet, assured trust that nothing can take away. This above all—this above all!

To *live* so that all my time may count for God and his Plan for my life—in business or pleasure, asleep or awake, in youth or age, in great things or small, to do the Father's will and in that will find my peace.

To *keep* alive the spiritual glow of true Christianity by prayer and devotions, Bible reading, grace at meals, systematic and unfailing attendance at church, fulfilling daily all spiritual duties.

To *advance* God's kingdom, beginning in my own life but moving at once to think and live for others in family, community, and nation—to right wrong, help the helpless, bind up the brokenhearted, give generously, love the brotherhood.

To *learn* through home and church and school and books and life's own experiences a richer wisdom as time goes by—that mind and soul, according well, may abound more and more in all knowledge and understanding, even to the understanding of the deep things of both man and God.

To *leave* to God the things I cannot know nor am meant to know, in sure and certain trust that he who created this world and called us into being, even the God and Father of our Lord Jesus Christ, will keep and perfect in his own time them that are his—in life, in death, in that vast forever. Even so, Father, keep thou us all.

INDEX

Communion, the Holy—*Cont'd*
  regulations for, 130
  Ritual for, 132-36
Conference:
  Annual, 100
  Annual Benevolence Budget, 153
  Central, 100
  Charge, 102
  Church, 120
  District, 102
  General, 96
  Jurisdictional, 98
Confession of Faith, 23
Confirmation, 137
"Connection," the, 11
Constitution, amendments to, 98
Constitutionality of legal decisions, 109
Conversion:
  Methodist belief regarding, 61-63
  Wesley's, 13
Costly apparel, wearing of, 81
Council, Judicial, 109
Council of Churches, 156
Council on Finance and Administration, 151
Council on Ministries, 104
Council, World Methodist, 165
Creed, Apostles', 23
Cup not denied laity, 53

Deacon:
  in Methodist polity, 114
  ordination of, 115
Deaconesses, 146
Decisions of law, 110
Delegates:
  Annual Conference, 100
  District Conference, 102
  General Conference, 96
  Jurisdictional Conference, 99
Diligence, rules regarding, 89

Discipline, Book of, 5, 97
Discipline, Methodist, 75
District:
  apportionments to, 153
  Committee on the Ministry, 112
  Conference, 102
  superintendent, 16
Diversions, rule regarding, 82
Divisions, Church:
  of the Evangelical Association, 22
  of the Methodist Episcopal Church, 19, 20
  of the United Brethren, 21
Doctrines:
  Bishops' statement on, 25
  of Methodism, 23-60, 61-74
  guidelines for, 24
Doing good, rules for, 85
Drinking spirituous liquors, 78
Du Bose, Bishop H. M. (quoted), 23

Ecumenical movement, 155
Education:
  Commission on (local church), 106
  Methodist, 19
Educational requirements for ministerial candidates, 112, 113
Elders:
  at Christmas Conference, 17
  ordination of, 115
Election:
  of bishops, 99
  of stewards and trustees, 118, 119
Embury, Philip, 14
Episcopacy, Methodist, 17, 117
Episcopal address, 97
Episcopal fund, 151
Episcopalians, relations with, 158

171

Evangelical Association, 22
Evangelical United Brethren, The, 22
Evangelism and Methodism, 72, 73
Examinations of ministerial candidates, 112, 113
Executive powers of Charge Conference, 103
Expenses, General Conference, 151
Experience as a guide, 25, 26
Experience meetings, 11, 13
Experiential religion, 10, 13

Falling from grace, 68
Family prayer, 92
Fasting, 93
Fifty-two sermons of Wesley, 23
Finance, church, 105, 150
Finance, Commission on (local church), 105
Financial plan (local church):
apportionments, 107
benevolences, 150
budget, 107
official responsibility for, 107
of United Methodist Women, 147
First Methodist Society, 10
Formality, Methodist fear of, 160
Free Will, article on, 38
Full connection, minister in (definition), 113
Funds:
Annual Conference, 150
District Conference, 150
Episcopal, 151
General Administration, 151
Interdenominational Cooperation, 152
Jurisdictional, 150

Funds—*Cont'd*
local church, 150
World Service, 151
Funerals as duty of pastor, 116

General Administration Fund, 151
General Conference:
composition of, 96
election of delegates to, 96
limitations on, 98
powers and duties of, 97
General Confession, 133
General Rules:
meaning of, 76
origin of, 75
General superintendents. *See* Bishops.
Gold, wearing of, 81
Golden Rule cited, 81
Good works, article on, 42
Goods, a Christian man's, 58
Growth:
of the Evangelical Association, 22
of Methodism, 18, 19
of The United Brethren, 21

Harrell, Bishop C. J. (quoted), 148
Heck, Barbara, 14
Holy Club, 10
Holy Communion, 130
Holy Ghost, article regarding, 32
Holy Scripture, article regarding, 34-36
Hymnal, The Methodist, 125, 126
Hymns, singing of, 13, 126

Interdenominational Cooperation Fund, 152
Interdenominational relations:
Division on Ecumenical and